$\mathcal{S}$ILK RIBBON EMBROIDERY

SILK RIBBON EMBROIDERY

Beautiful projects and elegant design ideas

Sheena Cable

Reader's Digest

THE READER'S DIGEST ASSOCIATION, INC.
Pleasantville, N.Y. • Montreal

A READER'S DIGEST BOOK

Created and produced by
Rosemary Wilkinson Publishing

The credits and acknowledgements that appear on page 128 are hereby
made a part of this copyright page.

Text Copyright © 1996 New Holland (Publishers) Ltd
Photography Copyright © 1996 New Holland (Publishers) Ltd
Illustrations Copyright © 1996 New Holland (Publishers) Ltd
Silk ribbon designs © 1996 Sheena Cable

First published in Great Britain in 1996 by New Holland (Publishers) Ltd

Library of Congress Cataloging in Publication Data
Cable, Sheena.
Silk Ribbon Embroidery: beautiful projects and elegant design ideas/Sheena Cable.
p. cm.
Includes index.
ISBN O-89577-934-X
I. Silk Ribbon Embroidery I. Title.
TT778.S64C33 1997
748.44--dc20

Printed and bound in Singapore.

CONTENTS

Introduction	6
First Steps	8
Stitch Library	14
The Projects:	
Laurel Wreath Cushion	30
Barrel Cushion	34
Lacy Bed Cushion	37
Heart-shaped Bed Pillow	40
Thai Silk Cushion	44
Pillowcase & Sheet	50
Pelmet & Tiebacks	53
Tablecloth & Napkins	58
Muslin Hat	61
Sunflower Hatband	64

Chinese Linen Blouse	67
Evening Wrap	70
Evening Vest	73
Gift Box	77
Padded Picture Frame	83
Christening Gown	87
Four Greeting Cards	91
Picture Bow	98
Folk Quilt Sampler	102
Rose Gift Box	107
Spiral Topiary Tree	110
Round Topiary Tree	114
Flower Garden Sampler	118
Index	127
Acknowledgments	128

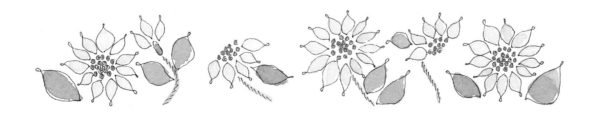

$\mathcal{I}$NTRODUCTION

When I was asked to write this book, there were certain things I immediately thought about that were very important to me. First, I wanted to make the instructions to my projects as easy to follow as possible and make them accessible to everyone. So to the step-by-step details for stitching and making up the pieces, I have added Notes and Tips in various places to give extra pointers to success.

Second, I wanted the book to have something for everyone. Therefore the projects cover different degrees of ability. For example, the Barrel Cushion on page 34 can be made by the absolute beginner. But other projects, such as the Round Topiary Tree on page 114, pose a bit of a challenge. Since silk ribbon embroidery has experienced a revival in some countries in just the last few years, I have tried to make most of the projects easy enough for people with little or no previous experience. You will find it most helpful to read the opening chapters on both the materials and the methods before you start to do any embroidery. However tempting it may be to get going straightaway on a project that has caught your eye, a little preparation is really worth the effort. The following chapter contains illustrated instructions for making all the stitches contained in the projects.

As you will see from flicking through the pages, I have covered a varied range of projects from table linen to simple greeting cards, hatbands to quilted samplers. I hope that within these pages you will find not only something that attracts your eye but also something that

may become useful to you. Perhaps that unusual and very personal Christening or wedding gift that you have searched the shops for is here in my book: an heirloom item that if cared for, can be handed down for a number of generations.

Silk ribbon embroidery, or Rococo embroidery as it was also known, started in France about 1750. It was used extensively in the French courts on the gowns worn at that time. Very shortly afterward it was brought to England for the same purpose.

From Great Britain silk ribbon embroidery was taken to America, Australia, and New Zealand. The Americans started to cultivate mulberry trees in order to produce their own silk, but the Orient was able to produce a much cheaper and more plentiful supply of silk, so now most of our silk ribbons come from the Far East.

In the late 1800s the art made one of its many revivals. At that time beautiful variegated ribbons were being produced in France and used throughout Great Britain and America.

Silk ribbon embroidery has gone in and out of fashion since the 1800s. The Victoria and Albert Museum in London has some fine examples both on display and in its reference section. One very pretty example is an English bag in black velvet, dated 1840. It is embroidered in silk ribbon and crepe gauze. The work is very delicate and has survived beautifully through time.

Throughout the late 1800s, articles in ladies' magazines gave ideas for the use of ribbon embroidery; many

suggested using it with lace and satin ribbons on parasols, evening bags, ball gowns, and the like.

The Victorians enjoyed a huge revival of the art. They used it with many other materials, such as beads, lace, and buttons, and they worked it onto many different pieces, including fire screens, gloves, hats, evening bags, and garments. Photography became very popular, so in order to display their treasured family photos, the Victorian ladies worked elaborate embroidery with silk ribbons, lace, and beads onto lush fabric to be made into picture frames.

The current revival of silk ribbon embroidery started around 1987 in Australia and has swept through both Australia and America. It is now becoming very popular in Britain. The wide selection of silk ribbons available in a fabulous palette of colors makes the art accessible to all. You can start off with just a small piece of fabric and a few ribbons. The style of contemporary work varies from period style to abstract. And as you will see from this book, it can be used on many things, from clothing to bedding and table linen. I sincerely hope the art of silk ribbon embroidery will not die out this time. I myself intend to do everything I can to help it remain with us.

Sherana Cassy

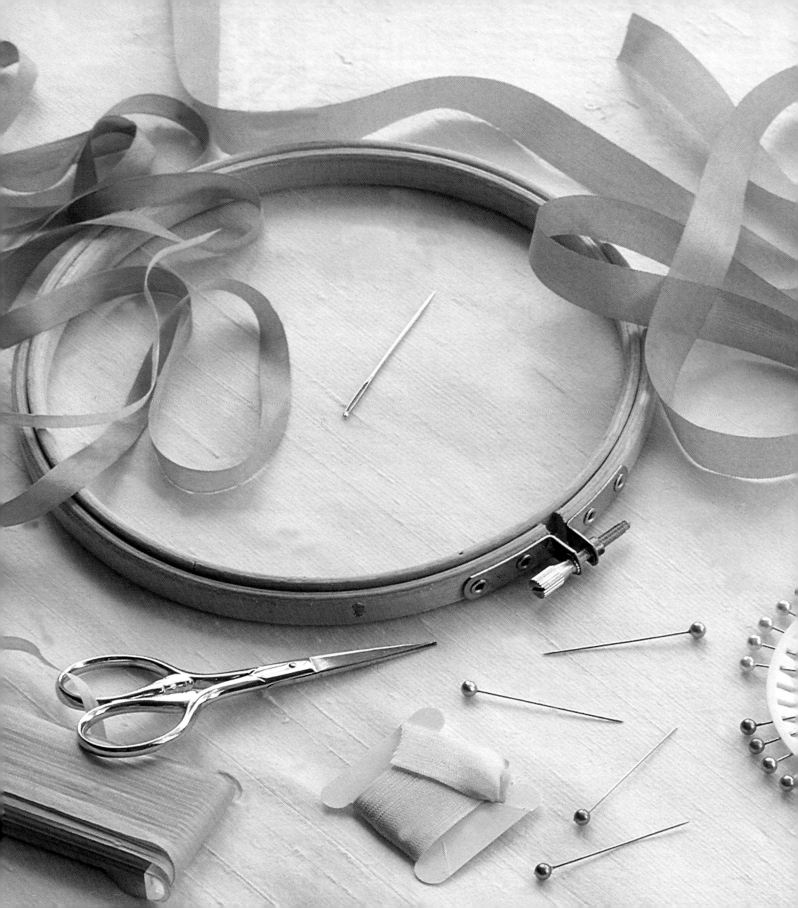

FIRST STEPS

Needles

You will need chenille needles for embroidering with silk ribbon, for they have a large eye. My favorite needle is a chenille No. 18. There are other sizes of chenille needles, but the thickness of the No. 18 needle works all the stitches in all the widths of ribbon beautifully. For the embroidery floss work you can use any embroidery needle you feel most comfortable with. A crewel needle with a sharp point and of medium length is the most popular choice.

Other work items

There are a few other essential items. To start with, you do need to work with your fabric in a frame or hoop of some description to keep the fabric taut so that you can judge the correct tension for the stitches. For the projects in this book I have used embroidery hoops of varying sizes, from a 5in to a 12in/13 to 30cm. The size of the project really determines the size of the hoop. My favorite size is a 8in/20cm. It accommodates most of the stitching motifs, and for projects in this book where the hoop size is not specified, it is more than likely that I have used a 8in/20cm hoop.

A plastic clip frame can be used instead of a hoop. It works well because it doesn't mark the fabric and is nice and chunky to hold in your hand. On a couple of occasions for larger items, I have used a tapestry frame. The choice of hoop or frame really comes down to personal preference. Choose the thing you are most comfortable working with.

Pins are always required. So is a sharp dressmaker's marking pencil in a pale color or tailor's chalk. A tape measure with both customary and metric measures is an essential. And lastly you will need a pair of sharp embroidery scissors.

Ribbons

Throughout most of this book, with the odd exception (where noted), I have used pure silk ribbon. Pure silk ribbon has a feel all its own. It lends itself beautifully to the production of flower petals and foliage: as in nature, no two petals are ever the same. Silk ribbon comes in various widths: 2mm; 4mm; 7mm; 13mm and 32 mm: 4mm tends to be the most popular and widely used. The narrower ribbons are used for smaller details and more delicate work.

There are now a number of man-made ribbons on the market and I have stitched with some of them for this book. I particularly like working with the variegated ribbons because these were the type (in silk) originally used to embroider French court dress in the 18th century. Man-made ribbons definitely have a place in the ribbon embroidery world. I would recommend, however, that you use only those that have been specifically manufactured for embroidery work to avoid any disappointment when washing your finished work.

I also use double-edged satin ribbon to make roses and wire-edged ribbon for bows and sometimes for roses on display work that I know will never be washed.

Quantities

You can now buy silk ribbon in handy pre-wound bobbin packs, usually measuring between 2 and 5 yards/2 to 5 meters.

To avoid disappointment, I would always recommend you buy half a yard (½ meter) more than the project suggests, because not everyone works with the same tension or to the same scale.

Other threads

Six-strand embroidery floss is used to add detail to silk ribbon work and to provide the basis for some of the silk ribbon stitches, such as the spider's web rose. Only small amounts are needed, especially since you usually work with only two strands at a time. But it is useful to have a range of colors to match the ribbons. The chief use of the floss is to add stalks and stems to floral designs, so a good selection of shades of green is particularly useful.

Pearl cotton (perle cotton) is a thicker thread than the embroidery floss but is used in the same way.

Gold thread is also used to add highlights to a silk ribbon design.

Beads

Beads are a natural embellishment for silk ribbon embroidery. I have used small pearl and glass beads in this book, but you could also use bugle bead.

Fabrics

I would thoroughly recommend that the beginning silk ribbon embroiderer go out and buy ½yd/50cm of muslin fabric. I love muslin. It has an open weave, and it stretches well on a frame. It is the perfect fabric for the novice to start with.

Many other fabrics lend themselves to silk ribbon work: damask, linen, cotton, moiré taffeta, velvet, and of course silk. I have tried to use a large variety of fabrics in this book to show how well the embroidery adapts to each fabric. Sheers and stretchy fabrics are not suitable for this kind of embroidery.

Laundering

Silk ribbon embroidery can be washed successfully. If you plan to work with strong colored ribbons on a light fabric, it is advisable to pre-wash the ribbons. Just a short soak in cold, salted water will be enough to wash out any surplus dye and set the remaining color. Alternatively, you can wash the ribbons in a mild detergent.

I have found it is worthwhile to ascertain ahead of time whether the fabric I use will shrink or not. Either check at the store where you bought it, or cut out a 3in/8cm square and pre-wash it in detergent.

Once you have finished a project, you may need to wash it. The best way I have found is to place the item in either an old pillowcase or a stocking holder and wash it in the machine at low temperature (woolen wash), using a mild detergent. Do not spin or tumble-dry the item; simply hang it out to air-dry. If the embroidery looks a little flat when dry, just spray it with a little water and it will pop back into shape. Then all you have to do is iron the item, avoiding the embroidery.

Stitch diagrams and templates

Stitch diagrams are given for most of the projects in this book. Where a full-size diagram is given, it can be transferred directly to the fabric. To do this, I suggest that you make a copy on tracing paper, then use a dressmaker's marking pencil to transfer it to the fabric. Or you

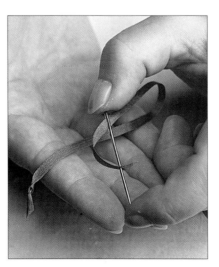

could just mark it out free-hand if you prefer. An exact copy is not important. Where templates are given, trace the outline onto thin poster board or template plastic and cut it out. Then draw around the template onto the fabric with tailor's chalk or marking pencil.

Starting off

When working with silk ribbons you must always cut them on the bias (diagonally) to avoid fraying. Work with short lengths of ribbon: no longer than 10in/25cm for the narrow (2 and 4mm) ribbons and even shorter lengths for the wider ribbons; otherwise, the ribbon will fray and run.

I recommend that you secure the thread onto the needle. To do this, first thread the ribbon through the eye of the needle leaving a tail of about ⅜in/9mm, then stab the point of the needle through the ribbon as shown in the photograph. Now take hold of the long tail of ribbon and gently pull the ribbon down until it locks onto the eye of the needle. All that remains then is to tie a knot at the end of the ribbon and you are now ready to begin.

Tension

When completing a stitch, allow the ribbon to lie relaxed on the surface of the background fabric, rather than pulling it taut. In this way the ribbon will form its own soft shapes.

Finishing off

When you have finished a length of ribbon, bring it to the back of your work and trim off the end diagonally. Now thread a crewel needle with sewing thread and attach to the loose piece of ribbon. Do not sew it down to the fabric because it may be seen from the front of your work. Just work a few stitches to secure the loose end to a previously worked stretch of ribbon, then cut the thread. It is better that you finish off each area of work rather than carry the ribbon across the back of the fabric to another area, since it is too easy to catch the ribbon and spoil the work that you have already completed.

Pinning ribbon

When working a bow or a curved line of ribbon, I always pin the ribbon very firmly in position first. It is important that the pins are close

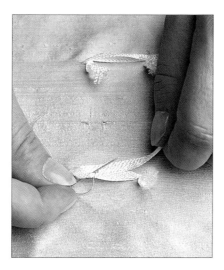

together to prevent the ribbon from being disturbed. It is impossible to reposition the ribbon once it has been stitched down.

Stitching beads

You will need to use a beading needle—which has a long, very thin shaft—since the holes in seed pearls and small glass beads are very small indeed. When stitching a number of beads to my work, I tend to use a sort of running stitch: I do not finish off after each bead but bring the needle up through the fabric, through the bead, down through the fabric, then back up again and through the next bead, and so on until the correct number of beads have been attached.

Making a tassel

Giving details on how to make a tassel can get technical. Describing warp and weft and the like and outlining how to use a jig can be complicated. In this book, I have worked very simple tassels, using the simplest of materials and implements: embroidery floss, a piece of sturdy cardboard and a pair of scissors.

First, decide on the length of the tassel you want and cut a piece of cardboard to that length and about 2½in/6cm wide. Take the embroidery floss and wrap it round the cardboard lengthwise approximately 20 to 30 times; the more times you wrap, the fuller the tassel will be.

Cut the thread, then cut a small length of the same floss and thread it onto a needle. Pass the needle under the floss on the cardboard at the top edge and take half the thread through. Remove the needle and tie the thread very tightly, to gather up the top of the tassel.

Cut the floss from the cardboard along the bottom edge, then take another length of floss and tie it round the tassel about ⅜in/1cm from the top, wrapping the thread three or four times before tying off. Trim the bottom to neaten it.

STITCH LIBRARY

This section contains all the silk ribbon embroidery stitches used in the projects throughout the book. The photographs show the stages in making the stitches as well as the finished stitch with its correct tension. I've included my hands in some of the photographs where it's important to see how to hold the ribbon or needle.

It's worth practicing these stitches on scraps of material, or you could make up your own stitch sampler in the same way as the Flower Garden Sampler on page 118. Details are often added with embroidery floss. Stem stitch is the most common, but backstitch and fly stitch are also often used. These stitches are given at the end of the Stitch Library. There are also instructions for a rose using satin ribbon.

Please note that in order to provide a cleaner photo, I have shortened the length of the ribbon when making some of the stitches. All your stitches should be worked normally: start with a 10in/25cm length as described on page 12.

Straight Stitch ▶
This is a universal stitch used for petals, in basket weave (as in the Topiary Tree projects on pages 110 and 114), and in abstract or geometric designs.

1 Bring the needle up through the fabric. Hold the ribbon straight against the fabric away from the direction in which you wish to work the stitch, by keeping it fairly taut with a second needle held in your other hand.
2 Take the needle back down into the fabric at the point that is correct for your stitch length, still holding the second needle under the ribbon to prevent the ribbon from twisting. Pull the ribbon through until the stitch is fairly taut but not so tight as to pucker the fabric.
3 The finished stitch should lie perfectly flat on the fabric. Sometimes, however, you actually want to work a twisted straight stitch. In that case, add the twist to the ribbon before holding it taut with the second needle.

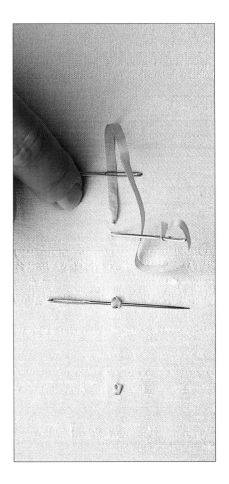

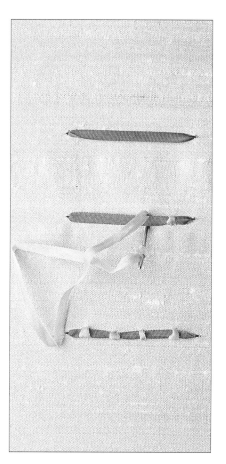

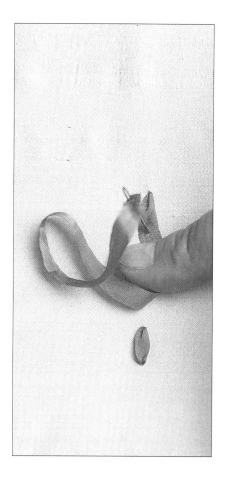

the ribbon over the existing ribbon and back down under the ribbon. Make the stitch quite firm.

3 Carry on along the length of the ribbon, spacing the couching out as evenly as possible. Note that in the photograph I have left the couching quite loose so that you can see the work clearly. The firmer the top stitch, the more gathered the stitch will become.

Ribbon Stitch ▶

I think this is possibly the most popular and most widely used stitch of all: for petals, leaves, and abstract work.

1 Bring the needle up through the fabric at the point that will be the base of the leaf or petal. Lay the ribbon onto the fabric in the direction in which you wish the stitch to go. Holding the ribbon down, pierce the ribbon in the center at the length you wish the stitch to be. Take the needle down through the ribbon and the fabric.

2 Pull the ribbon through until you get a roll, then very carefully pull through slowly until you have a leaf shape. If you pull the ribbon

Couched Straight Stitch ▲

This stitch can be worked as a border to edge a piece of embroidery or to work an initial.

1 Work one straight stitch (see page 16) to the length required either vertically or horizontally.

2 With either the same color ribbon or a contrasting color, come up underneath the ribbon. Take

through too far, you will end up with a thin line of ribbon that is unfortunately irretrievable. The key to this stitch is to work it very slowly.

3 To make a puffed ribbon stitch, instead of laying the ribbon flat, push it back toward the point at which you brought the needle out, then take the needle down through the ribbon as before.

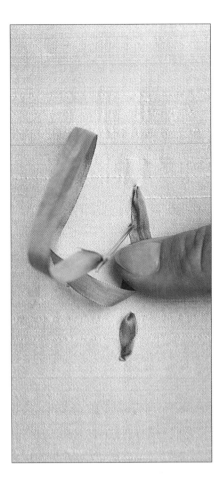

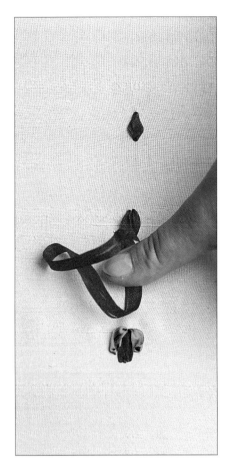

a side ribbon stitch or the slightly fatter shape of a ribbon stitch.

1 This stitch is worked exactly the same as the ribbon stitch except that you pierce the ribbon at the left- or right-hand side before taking the needle back down into the fabric.
2 The working of this stitch creates an interesting twist, or curve, to the stitch and is great for leaves and petals. You can choose to curve the stitch to the right or to the left, depending which side of the ribbon you pierce.

Back-to-back Ribbon Stitch ▶
This stitch is wonderful for working rosebuds. And as the photograph shows, with a smaller ribbon stitch worked in green on either side, it looks very realistic.

1 Work one ribbon stitch in the normal manner (see page 17).
2 Work a second ribbon stitch next to the first stitch, starting at the bottom as near to the first stitch as possible. I tend to work both of these using side ribbon stitch so that the top points of the stitch sit back-to-back more

Side Ribbon Stitch ▲
This stitch is used instead of the ribbon stitch on page 17 when you wish to give a particular slant to a stitch. When to use ribbon stitch and when side ribbon stitch on a flower head is a matter of personal choice. Once you have worked a few petals in ribbon stitch, you will be able to judge whether the space left is better suited to the curve of

closely. Take your time with this stitch; it is very easy to pierce the first stitch while working the second.

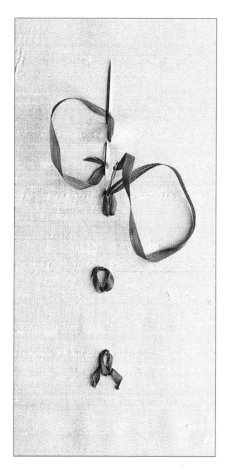

the stitch, keeping the loop of the ribbon underneath the point of the needle.

2 Pull the ribbon through the fabric until the loop is the required size. Do not pull it too tight. To anchor the loop, take the needle back down into the fabric just the other side of the loop.

3 To turn this into a simple iris, bring the needle up again slightly below and to the right of the bottom of the stitch. Turn the needle around and go under the chain (needle eye first), then pull the ribbon through fairly loosely. Take the needle back down into the fabric at the same distance from the bottom of the lazy daisy stitch at the left-hand side. Chain stitch is formed when the lazy daisy stitches are worked in an unbroken line.

Lazy Daisy Stitch/Chain Stitch ▲

This stitch is used for flowers, particularly irises, for leaves, petals, and abstract work.

1 Bring your needle up through the fabric. Pull the ribbon through and loop it round. Take the needle back down through the fabric next to where the ribbon emerges, then up again at the desired length of

Blocked Lazy Daisy Stitch ▶

As its name implies, this is a solid version of the open lazy daisy stitch described above.

1 Work one lazy daisy stitch as previously shown. Bring the needle up at the bottom of the stitch and

make a loose single straight stitch through the middle.

2 The center stitch can be worked in the same color as the lazy daisy or in a contrasting shade.

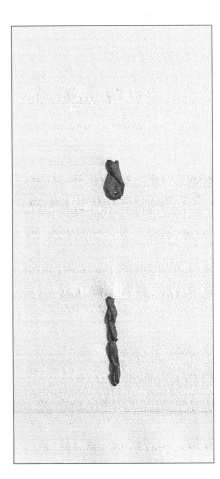

require the stitch to be, with the ribbon looped around the top of the needle. At this point, before you pull the needle through, take hold of the loop and twist it to form a figure eight over the needle. Pull the ribbon through, then take the needle back down above the third stitch to secure.

2 Bring the needle up just above the first stitch and repeat until you reach the required length of chain.

Merrilyn Bow ▶

This bow was developed by Merrilyn Heazlewood, a top silk ribbon designer and teacher. It is especially suitable on projects that are likely to be laundered regularly.

1 Using any width of ribbon and working from the center of the bow out, work one large lazy daisy stitch (see page 19) horizontally to the left of the center. The size of the lazy daisy stitch is of course determined by the size of the bow you require.

2 Work a second lazy daisy stitch horizontally to the right of the center. Then bring the needle back out at the center again and work

Twisted Chain Stitch ▲

A useful linear stitch that can be worked in a straight line or curved.

1 Bring the needle up through the fabric, loop the ribbon around from left to right, then take the needle back down next to the point at which you came up. Come up again through the fabric above the first two points at the length you

one long stitch downward to form one of the bow tails.

3 Take the needle back to the center, come up through the fabric and work a second tail. Make this tail a different length from the first, and if you like (I think it looks better), add a twist to the tails. Go back up to the center again and work a small diagonal straight stitch over the center of the bow.

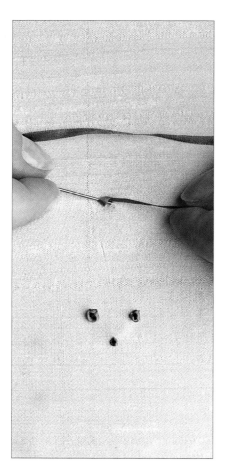

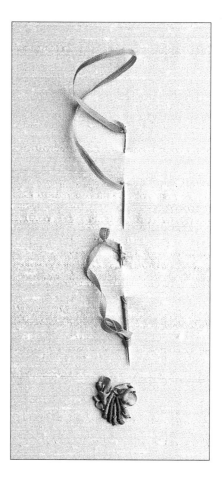

2 Take the needle back down into the fabric as near as you can to where you came up.

You can regulate the tension and ultimately the size of the knot by holding the ribbon in your other hand and keeping it either fairly taut or loose around the needle.

Bullion Stitch ▶

This stitch can be used to form flowers and for abstract designs. Since it is firmly secured to the fabric, it is a good stitch for working on garments or bedding, where laundering will be frequent.

1 Bring your needle up through the fabric, noting that this point will be the top of your bullion knot. Take the needle back down into the fabric at the required length of the stitch, then back up again as near to the point where you first came up as possible without going into the same hole. Do not pull the needle right through the fabric, only about halfway.
2 Take the ribbon and wrap it around the needle as many times as necessary so that it will cover the length of the stitch required.

French Knot ▲

This is used for the centers of flowers and is excellent for greenery in clusters. It is also used for securing scrolls of ribbon to the background fabric.

1 Bring the needle up through the fabric. Twist the ribbon once around the point of the needle (twice for a bigger knot).

Gently pull the needle through the fabric and take it back down next to the bottom stitch. Pull the ribbon through very carefully until the bullion is lying close to the fabric.
3 Beautiful roses can be worked using bullions in harmonious colors surrounded at the base with petals in 7mm puffed ribbon stitch, as shown in the photograph.

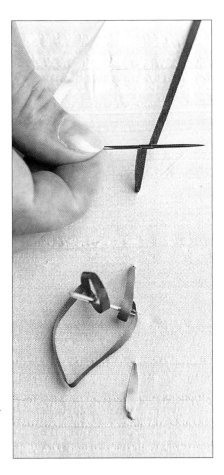

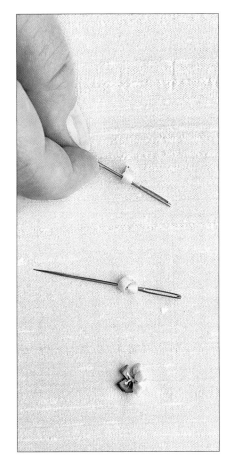

(see page 16), hold the ribbon away from the direction in which you want to go, using a second needle (this guides the ribbon and stops it from twisting as you stitch).

2 Before you take the needle back down into the fabric, wrap the ribbon around the needle (in the same way as for a French knot).

3 Take the needle down into the fabric, controlling the tension of the ribbon with your left hand (right, if you are left-handed).

Loop Stitch ▶

Worked in 4mm variegated ribbon, this makes an attractive flower.

1 Bring the needle up through the fabric at the center of the flower or at the point where you wish the finished loop to be. Make a loop over a second needle or a pencil, depending on the size you wish the finished loop to be. Take the needle back down into the fabric next to the start of the stitch, making the loop the desired size.

2 Come up through the fabric again close to the first stitch and make a second loop, passing the loop over the same needle or pencil

Pistil Stitch ▲

This stitch, as its name suggests, is wonderful for working the pistils on flower heads, but it can also be used in any abstract design. Its length is determined by the size of the flower being worked; the pistil must be in scale with the petals.

1 Bring the needle up through the fabric and, as in the straight stitch

to ensure that it is the same length as the first. Work around in a circle to make a flower, always keeping two loops on the needle or pencil to keep an even size throughout.

3 To finish off, you could either work two or three French knots in the center or work a pistil stitch (see left) in embroidery floss into the center of each loop, as shown in the photograph.

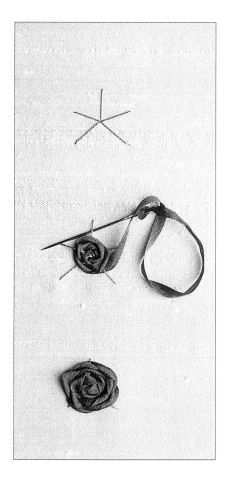

Spider Web Rose ▲

This is a good stitch to work on garments or household linen as it is firmly fixed to the fabric with no loops or loose ribbons. These roses look good either on their own or in a group with other flowers.

1 Work a spider web (five stitches), using two strands of embroidery floss in a color that matches the ribbon.

2 Now, using ribbon and starting at any point, come up through the fabric close to the web center. Take the needle under the first stitch of the web and over the next. Continue in this way, working alternately under and over the embroidery floss stitches. Keep the ribbon tension fairly loose and give it a slight twist with each stitch.

3 Continue working round and round until you reach the outside of the web. Take the ribbon back down through the fabric. This rose can look very attractive if worked well and in two different ribbons.

Coral Stitch ▶

A very pretty stitch used to form flower heads when worked in a circle as here, or it can be stitched in a line. Practice makes perfect with this one. I have used variegated ribbon, which adds to its charm.

1 Start with three French knots (see page 21) to form the center.

2 Bring the needle up on the right-hand side next to the French knots. Take the needle down and up again, pointing out from the center and wrap the ribbon over the top of the needle, then under the point of the needle. Pull the needle fully through the fabric.

3 Continue around the French knots for a complete round, then repeat to make a second round. Keep the stitches close together. The tension determines how loopy the stitch is, and you should try to keep the loops as even as possible.

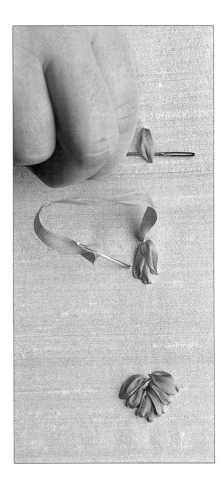

2 For the second stitch, bring the needle up at the bottom of the first stitch and go down into the fabric to the left and slightly below the top of the first stitch. Start the third stitch at the bottom of the second stitch and bring it out to the right of the first stitch. Take the needle down to the right and slightly below the top of the center stitch. Continue like this, working left, right, left, right, until the flower head is the size you require.

3 To finish off, as an option, as shown in the photograph, I have worked single stitches in a different color in between the main stitches, I have just tucked them behind the main stitches using the eye of a needle, to form a contrast and a little more interest.

Fishbone Stitch ▲

Used to work roses, this looks good in variegated ribbons.

1 You can work this in a line, but for the purpose of demonstration I have worked a flower head. Work one straight stitch to form the center of the flower. The length of the stitch determines the size of the flower.

Whipped Running Stitch ▶

This is a great stitch for defining shapes, forming words and neatening the edges of basketwork.

1 Work a row of running stitches in any shape to suit your pattern or design.

2 With a second ribbon (either the same or contrasting color), come up through the fabric at the end of the running stitches, then pass the needle underneath the first stitch from left to right (or vice versa if left-handed).

3 Work all along the running stitches in the same way, trying to keep the stitches smooth and the tension as even as possible. You could double-wrap each stitch for a more raised, rope effect if desired.

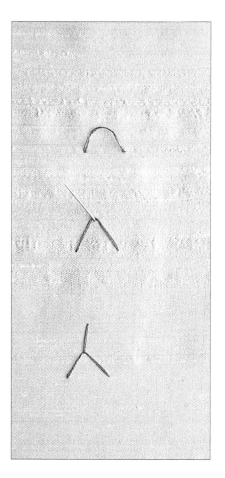

Pre-gathered Rose ▲

A pretty, full-blown rose, which can be worked with just one length of 7mm wide ribbon or with a second length of 4mm ribbon in a contrasting shade.

1 Cut a piece of ribbon 11in/ 28cm long or one length of 7mm and one of 4mm in another color. If using two ribbons, lay the 4mm ribbon on top of the 7mm with one edge aligned. Knot the end of the ribbons. Knot a length of sewing thread and sew through the ribbons at the knot end. Work a small running stitch through both ribbons along the edge.

2 Unthread, then rethread ribbons and sewing thread into a chenille needle. Come up through the fabric at the desired point. Un-thread the chenille needle and with a new length of thread and a small needle, come up through the fabric next to the ribbon. Gather a little of the ribbon at the fabric end and stitch down. Gather a little more and stitch down. Work round and round, gathering and stitching down, making the stitches underneath the previous round to get a tight ruffle.

3 When you are left with just 1½in/4cm of ribbon, re-thread the chenille needle and take the ribbon back down into the fabric just after the last stitch. Sew down at the back and cut off the tails.

Fly Stitch in Embroidery Floss ▶

A useful stitch for adding calyxes to flower heads.

1 This stitch is worked from top to bottom. Bring the needle up through the fabric. Take it back down to the right of the first stitch on the same line and, in the same movement, bring it up again through the fabric below but midway between the two stitches.

2 Pull the thread through and take the needle down into the fabric below the central stitch.

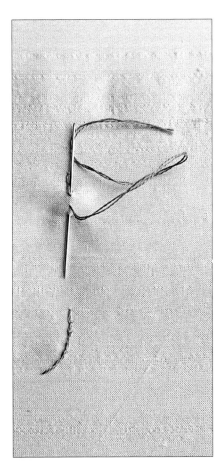

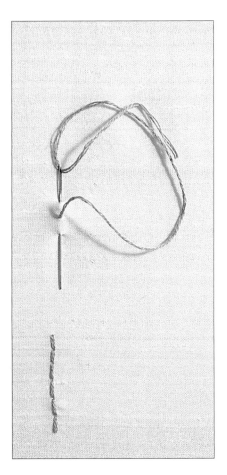

the fabric at the beginning of the placement for the stem or outline and work one single straight stitch. Bring the needle up again half a stitch length away in the direction of and exactly on the line of the stem. Take the needle down (working back on yourself) halfway along the length of the first stitch and just to one side of it, then bring it back up half a stitch length farther away.

2 Continue in this way until you reach the desired length of the stem or outline.

Backstitch in Embroidery Floss ▶

Backstitch makes a continuous line useful for outlining or adding detail to a design.

1 Bring the needle up through your fabric a stitch length away from your required starting point in the direction of working and go back down into the fabric at the starting point. Bring the needle back up a stitch length away from the start of the first stitch exactly on the line being worked and take it back down again next to the

Stem Stitch in Embroidery Floss ▲

This is a very useful stitch, not only for working stems to silk ribbon flowers but also for marking the outline of many shapes. You can curve the line of stitches (in any direction), or you can work it straight.

1 Bring your needle up through

point where your first stitch emerged.

2 Continue in this way until you reach your required length of work.

close to the end of the first stitch as possible.

2 Continue this way until you have filled the required area.

Double-edged Satin Rose ▶

Satin ribbon makes a three-dimensional rose that looks good either on its own or in a cluster. It is not easy to launder and so would not be used on clothing. To show up more clearly in the photograph, sewing thread in a contrasting color has been used, but you should of course use a matching color to obscure the securing stitches.

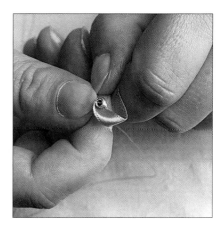

1 Take any width of double-edged satin ribbon. You will need about 20in/51cm per rose. You will also need a length of matching thread and a sharp-pointed embroidery needle. Cut the end of the ribbon on the cross and fold it down. Roll the ribbon around three times to make a firm tube and stitch into place at the bottom. Holding the roll in your right hand and the rest of the ribbon in your left hand, turn the ribbon back on itself and wrap it around the roll

in the right hand. Stitch into place.

2 Keep on folding the ribbon in the left hand and stitching it around the rose in the right hand until you feel the rose is the correct size.

3 To finish off, cut the ribbon on the cross and tuck it back on itself. Stitch down, then sew into place on the fabric.

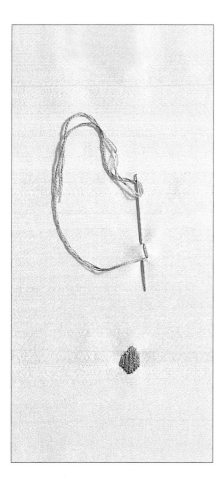

Satin Stitch in Embroidery Floss ▲

Usually used to fill in an area with solid color.

1 Bring the needle up through the fabric and take it down at the required length. Bring the needle up again as close to the start of the first stitch as possible, then take the needle back down again as

THE PROJECTS

LAUREL WREATH CUSHION

This cushion is an ideal beginner's project worked on muslin, a fabric that is very simple to handle and easy to embroider. I was inspired by the classical laurel leaf motif for the embroidery to finish the cushion with a gathered and knotted border as an echo of a Roman toga.

YOU WILL NEED

1⅓yd/1.2m unbleached muslin, 45in/114cm wide

3⅓yd/3m 7mm emerald green silk ribbon

Embroidery hoop or frame

Tailor's chalk or dressmaker's marking pencil

No. 18 chenille needle

Crewel or similar needle

Matching green embroidery floss

16in/41cm cushion pad

Matching sewing thread

Diagonal stitch

Ribbon stitch

French knot

To stitch the design

1 Muslin is likely to shrink when washed, so it is best that you pre-wash the fabric. Since you will also want to launder the embroidery, soak the ribbon in cold, salted water before using. This will prevent the dye from running in any subsequent washes.

2 Press the fabric carefully to make certain that all the creases are removed; you cannot

iron over the embroidery once you have finished the piece.

3 Cut a square of muslin, 17¼ x 17¼in/43 x 43cm and stretch it on an embroidery hoop or frame. Mark the center of your fabric with two crossed pins or a tailor's chalk cross.

4 Working from the center, draw a circle 8in/20cm in diameter with either a pencil or tailor's chalk. Mark the center top and bottom of the circle with a vertical pin.

5 Using the green silk ribbon, bring the needle up through the fabric about 1¼in/3cm to the left of the bottom center pin. Lay the ribbon in a diagonal line of 2¾in/7cm, then take the needle down into the fabric, forming one diagonal straight stitch (do not pull the ribbon tight). Repeat this stitch,

this time bringing the needle up 1¼in/3cm to the right of the bottom center pin. Lay the ribbon on top of the first stitch and take it to the back of the fabric to make the second diagonal stitch, crossing over the first.

6 Starting ⅜in/1cm up the left-hand side (see stitch diagram on page 30), work pairs of ribbon

stitch leaves around the edge of the circle. As you work round the circle, decrease the size of the leaves very slightly. Stop about ¾in/2cm from the top center pin, then work a single leaf at a slight angle to the pencil circle, pointing upwards.

7 Repeat Step 6 to work all the way up the right-hand side of the circle.

NOTES AND TIPS

Do not worry about whether there is an equal number of leaf sets on either side of the wreath; it will not be noticeable. Be more concerned with forming the ribbon stitch leaves correctly.

8 To finish off the design, pin the two diagonal stitches at the bottom of the wreath so that they curve a little to give the effect of a bow. Then, using two strands of the embroidery floss, attach the ribbons to the fabric with evenly spaced French knots. Remove the pins as you work.

To make the cushion

The cushion cover is slip stitched together and can be unpicked for laundering. A zipper could be fitted if desired, but this cushion is really intended to be decorative rather than hardwearing.

1 From the remaining muslin, cut a piece 17¼in/43cm square.

2 Place the square on top of the embroidered piece with right sides together and machine-stitch around the sides, taking $^5/_8$in/1.5cm seam allowance and leaving a gap in one side large enough to insert the cushion pad into. Trim the corners and turn right side out. Do not bother to push out the corners; leave them rounded.

3 Insert the cushion pad and slip stitch the sides of the gap together.

4 From the remaining muslin, make up a strip 8in/20cm wide and the length of the circumference of the cushion plus an extra 26in/66cm. Make this piece into a tube by stitching down one long side with a $^5/_8$in/1.5cm seam, right sides together, then turning it right side out.

5 Place one end of the tube just to the right of the bottom right-hand corner and pin it to the cushion. Take the tube along to the bottom left-hand corner, then tie the tube into a loose knot, so that it sits on the corner (see Diagram 1). Pin in place. Stitch the tube to the

cushion, matching the seams but leaving the first 4in/10cm unattached. Repeat the process on the next two corners and stitch the tube down completely.

6 Make the fourth knot next to the third knot. Tuck one raw end of the tube inside the other, ensuring that the tube closely fits the final side of the cushion. Turn under a narrow hem on the visible raw end and slip stitch in position (see Diagram 2). Work the fourth knot along the tube until it lies over the final corner; the join should then disappear into the knot. Stitch the remaining side of the tube down to the cushion.

VARIATION

If you add a zipper, insert it across the middle of the cushion cover back, allowing extra fabric for seams.

Diagram 1

Diagram 2

BARREL CUSHION

Barrel cushions always look so elegant on a sofa or a chaise longue. On this one I have worked an abstract design that will look good in any modern living room. This is a simple project suitable for a beginner. It can be stitched on a store-bought cushion if preferred.

YOU WILL NEED

I barrel cushion including pad

or

A barrel cushion pad and enough fabric to cover the pad; see below (I have used a self-striped damask type fabric.)

Tailor's chalk or dressmaker's marking pencil

Embroidery hoop or frame

No. 18 chenille needle

2¾yd/2.5m 4mm ginger brown silk ribbon

2¼yd/2m 4mm light olive green silk ribbon

2¼yd/2m 4mm dark olive green silk ribbon

I skein ginger brown embroidery floss

matching sewing thread

To stitch the design

1 For the cushion cover you will need three pieces of fabric, measured as follows:

* the length of the barrel cushion pad x the circumference plus ⅝in/1.5cm seam allowance all around;

* two circles the same size as the cushion pad ends plus seam allowances as before.

2 Working on the barrel of the cushion, measure 3in/7.5cm from each end and draw a line in chalk or pencil. Stretch the fabric in a hoop or frame.

3 Because I was working on striped fabric, I was able to work one pattern on each alternate stripe. If you choose to work on plain fabric, then you just need to space each pattern equally at a distance of approximately 1¼ in/3cm, being sure to keep clear of the seam allowances.

4 For each pattern, draw a V that measures 1¼ in/3cm high and 1in/2.5cm between its widest parts. (See stitch diagram below.)

Couched straight stitch	
French knot	
Lazy daisy stitch	

5 Using the ginger ribbon, work the V shape in two long straight stitches.

6 Using the light olive ribbon, couch the ginger ribbon in two places at each side of the V. But couch the ribbon loosely so that the ginger ribbon stays straight.

7 Using the dark olive ribbon, work one French knot at the end of each ginger straight stitch.

8 With the same ribbon, work one lazy daisy stitch at the point of each V.

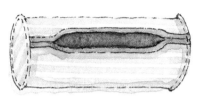

9 Work the opposite end of the barrel in the same way. But you can, like me, reverse the direction of the Vs if you prefer.

10 To work the ends of the cushion, find the center and mark it with crossed pins. Mark four V shapes the same size as previously worked on the barrel, all with the points inward. Leave a small gap in the very center.

11 Work the four Vs in the same way as before without the lazy daisy stitch at the points.

12 Using the embroidery floss, make a very simple tassel (see page 13) and stitch it into the center of the four Vs.

To make the cushion

1 Fold the piece for the barrel of the cushion in half lengthways,

right sides together, and pin the long edge. Machine-stitch for 2in/5cm at either end of this edge, taking a ⅝in/1.5cm seam allowance, thus leaving a gap large enough to insert the cushion pad.

2 Press the seam and the raw edges flat.

3 Pin one of the circle ends to the short edge of the barrel piece, with right sides together and raw edges aligned. Baste, then machine-stitch all around with the usual seam allowance.

4 Repeat at the other end (see diagram). Turn right side out. Insert the cushion pad, then slip stitch the gap together by hand.

LACY BED CUSHION

Scattering a selection of small cushions on your bed always gives it a more luxurious look. This small square cushion can be easily made with a knowledge of only three stitches. It uses double-edged satin ribbon for the first time. While this is not suitable for the embroidered stitches, it is very good for making the twisted roses. They cannot be laundered but are particularly suitable for purely decorative pieces.

YOU WILL NEED

A store-bought white cotton or silk cushion

or

A 12in/30cm square cushion pad and ½yd/46cm white cotton sheeting fabric, 64in/163cm wide, plus lace long enough to go around the cushion twice

Tailor's chalk or dressmaker's marking pencil

Embroidery hoop or frame

No. 18 chenille needle

Crewel or similar needle

Light green embroidery floss

1⅓yd/1.5m ⅜in/9mm double-edged dark pink satin ribbon

Dark pink sewing thread (to match satin ribbon)

1⅔yd/1.5m 7mm light green silk ribbon

White sewing thread

To stitch the design

1 If making your own cushion, cut two squares of sheeting, both measuring 13in/33cm per side. Using chalk or pencil, mark a 12in/30cm square centrally on the right side of one of the squares. Draw a diagonal line from corner to corner of the marked square. Repeat to make a diagonal in the opposite direction. Next draw a series of lines, parallel to each diagonal, each line to be 1¾in/4.5cm away from the last. Work out to the corners of the square so that the whole of the marked area is covered in a lattice.

2 If you are working with a store-bought cushion cover, draw the lattice on one side as described in Step 1, taking the lines right up to the edges.

3 Stretch the marked square on an embroidery hoop or frame. Using two strands of the green embroidery floss, work all the lattice pattern in stem stitch. Try to keep your stitches as even and straight as possible.

4 With the dark pink satin ribbon, make 13 double-edged satin roses.

5 Stitch the roses securely onto the lattice in the positions shown in the photograph below.

6 Using the green silk ribbon, work ribbon stitch and side ribbon stitch leaves around the roses. Vary the number of leaves and the positions with each rose.

To make the cushion

1 Join the lace into a circle by stitching the two short ends, right sides together, with a ⅜in/1cm seam.

2 Gather the lace to half its original length along the top of the straight edge. Place on top of the embroidered square, with right sides together, so that the gathered line of the lace lies on top of the marked stitching line. Pin in place, adjusting the gathers so that they lie evenly but with extra fullness at the corners (see diagram). Baste in place and remove pins.

3 Place the second square of cotton sheeting on top of the embroidered piece with right sides together and machine-stitch around

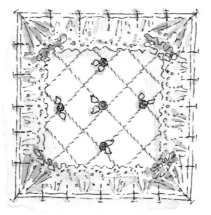

the sides, taking ⅝in/1.5cm seam allowance and leaving a gap in one side large enough to insert the cushion pad. Trim the corners and turn right side out.

4 Insert the cushion pad and slip stitch the sides of the gap together.

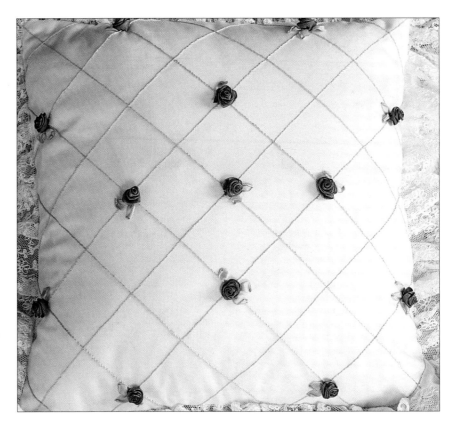

HEART-SHAPED BED PILLOW

Small pillows placed at the head of a bed can really add a touch of style and elegance. This small heart-shaped pillow is fairly simple to work yet looks quite involved to the untrained eye.

YOU WILL NEED

1yd/1m pink silk dupioni, 45in/114cm wide

Tailor's chalk or dressmaker's marking pencil

Embroidery hoop or frame

No. 18 chenille needle

Crewel or similar needle

Light pink embroidery floss

20in/51cm 4mm dark pink silk ribbon

20in/51cm 4mm medium pink silk ribbon

20in/51cm 4mm light pink silk ribbon

Light green embroidery floss

30in/76cm 4mm mauve silk ribbon

Lemon yellow embroidery floss

20in/51cm 4mm lavender silk ribbon

20in/51cm ¼in/6mm dusty pink silk ribbon

Gold embroidery floss

20in/51cm ¼in/6mm light green silk ribbon

20in/51cm 4mm dark green silk ribbon

Dark green embroidery floss

20in/51cm 3mm light green silk ribbon

Heart-shaped pillow pad

To stitch the design

1 Cut out two pieces of silk dupioni, 12in/30cm square. Then with tailor's chalk or pencil, and using the template on page 43, draw the shape of the embroidery onto the center of one of the squares. Stretch the fabric onto a hoop or frame.

2 Starting at the bottom, work three spider web roses in the position shown in the stitch diagram on page 42 as follows. Using two strands of light pink embroidery floss, work the web. Change to the dark pink ribbon, work two rounds of the web, and fasten off. Next work three rounds in medium pink, then finally two loose rounds in the light pink.

3 Work the buds in medium pink, using two side ribbon stitches back to back, then work the calyxes. Using the light green embroidery floss, first work a fly stitch around each bud, then a single straight stitch from the middle of each bud to its base, and finally a long straight stitch for the stalk.

4 Work all the tiny mauve flowers in small loop stitches, making three petals to each flower. Use two strands of lemon yellow embroidery floss to work the centers in French knots.

5 Work the little lavender flowers in ribbon stitch and side ribbon stitch (see the note on page 18).

6 Work the large roses in ¼in/6mm dusty pink ribbon, each with five petals in ribbon stitch. The rosebuds are also worked in ribbon stitch. There is a French knot in the middle and pistil stitches on each petal, all worked in two strands of gold embroidery floss.

7 Work the leaves of the spider web roses with ¼in/6mm light green ribbon in both ribbon stitch and side ribbon stitch.

8 Work the leaves of the lavender flowers in ⅛in/3mm dark green ribbon in ribbon stitch.

⬯	Side ribbon stitch
⬯	Ribbon stitch
∿	Stem stitch
�===ᶕ	Whipped running stitch
•—○	Pistil stitch
▽	Loop stitch
⊙	French knot
Ψ	Fly stitch and straight stitch
⊚	Spider web rose

9 To work the stems of the lavender flowers, use two strands of matching dark green embroidery floss and stem stitch with one or two straight stitches to attach the petals to the stem.

10 The final stage is to join up all the flower groups. Use ⅛in/3mm light green silk ribbon and work in whipped running stitch.

To make the cushion

1 Cut the two squares of fabric into heart shapes, using the cushion pad as a guide and adding a 1in/2.5cm seam allowance.

2 From the remaining silk fabric cut strips 6in/15cm wide and as long as possible. Join at the short edges to make one long strip.

3 Fold this strip in half lengthwise, then pin it to the right side of the embroidered piece, raw edges matching; make small pleats as you go (see diagram). About 4in/10cm from the end, cut the strip to the right length, then open

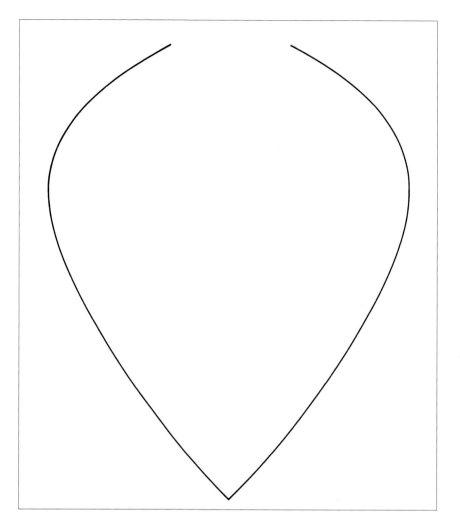

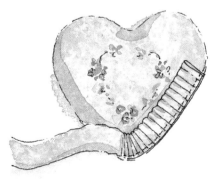

it out and stitch it to the start of the strip, right sides together. Finish pleating. Baste, then machine stitch in place.

4 Place the remaining heart-shaped piece of fabric on top of the embroidered piece, right sides together and with the edging still facing inward. Pin, baste, then machine-stitch over the previous stitching line, leaving a gap large enough to insert the cushion pad.

5 Turn right side out and pull out the pleated edging. Insert the pad, then slip stitch the edges of the gap together.

THAI SILK CUSHION

This beautiful Thai silk cushion instantly caught my eye in a department store, and I fell in love with the color and the fabric. I just knew I could work a design that would look great on this background. I started out with a simple bouquet design in mind, but the idea gradually developed into this rather ornate urn filled with all kinds of flowers. This is a project for the more advanced silk ribbon embroiderer.

YOU WILL NEED

Thai silk cushion (pad included), 16in/41cm square

Tailor's chalk or dressmaker's marking pencil

Embroidery hoop or frame

No. 18 chenille needle

Crewel or similar needle

30in/76cm 4mm light lavender silk ribbon

30in/76cm 4mm dark lavender silk ribbon

20in/51cm 7mm medium lavender silk ribbon

20in/51cm 7mm pale green silk ribbon

3½yd/3.2m 4mm dusty pink silk ribbon

3½yd/3.2m 4mm light dusty pink silk ribbon

40in/1m 7mm cerise silk ribbon

40in/1m 4mm cream silk ribbon

2¼yd/2m 4mm light pink silk ribbon

3½yd/3m 4mm mustard silk ribbon

3½yd/3m 4mm lemon silk ribbon

40in/1m 4mm dark turquoise silk ribbon

2¼yd/2m 4mm light turquoise silk ribbon

40in/1m 4mm lemon green silk ribbon

40in/1m 4mm pale moss green silk ribbon

20in/51cm 4mm dark green silk ribbon

2¼yd/2m 4mm moss green silk ribbon

Pale brown embroidery floss for foliage stalks

Pale green embroidery floss for rose and peony stems

Green embroidery floss for rosebud calyxes and stems

1 piece of bronze silk dupioni, 4½ x 5½in/11 x 14cm

Bronze sewing thread

Gold embroidery thread

1 brass cherub

Clear varnish

Fabric glue

Hot glue gun (optional)

To stitch the design

Mark the positions of all the main flowers, stems, and the urn on the center of the cushion front. Use tailor's chalk or pencil and follow the full size stitch diagram on page 48 and the template on page 49. Stretch the fabric on a hoop or frame.

2 Work the three peonies first. Using the light lavender ribbon, work one long lazy daisy stitch for the centre of the flower, then four or five ribbon stitches at the sides. Change to the dark lavender ribbon and work four or five twisted pistil stitches radiating out from the centre. Next using the 7mm medium lavender ribbon, work six ribbon stitches fanning out downwards and to the sides, then infill with ribbon stitch leaves in pale green ribbon.

3 Using the dusty and light dusty pink ribbon, work the two lilacs next in French knots. Mix the two colours randomly to give the flowers a shaded look.

4 Using the 7mm cerise ribbon, work the buds using ribbon stitch and side ribbon stitch.

5 Using the cream ribbon, work one lazy daisy stitch for the centre of each of the four roses with one side ribbon stitch on either side. Using the light pink ribbon, work two ribbon stitches at either side of the cream stitches, then one stitch slanting downwards.

6 Sew the five mustard flowers by starting with three French knots in mustard ribbon for the centres. Using the lemon ribbon, work twice round the knots in coral stitch, then once round the outside with the mustard ribbon, again in coral stitch.

7 To work the seven turquoise flowers, first work the centres with three French knots in the dark turquoise, then work round the knots with the light turquoise in lazy daisy stitches.

8 Using the lemon/green ribbon, work the foliage branches in ribbon and side ribbon stitches. Repeat for the leaves on the rose stalks using pale moss green ribbon.

9 Work all the remaining leaves on the flowers as follows: rosebud leaves in pale moss green ribbon in ribbon stitch; mustard flower leaves in dark green ribbon and ribbon stitch; two leaves on the left-hand peony stalk in 7mm pale green ribbon and ribbon stitch and the leaves for the turquoise flowers in moss green ribbon worked in lazy daisy stitch.

10 Work all the stalks in stem stitch using two strands of embroidery floss as in the list of materials, except the stalks and calyxes for the cerise buds. To work these, using two strands of embroidery floss, first work a fly stitch round each bud, then a single straight stitch from the middle of each bud to its base and finally a long straight stitch for the stalk.

11 Transfer the outline of the urn given in the template to the bronze silk using chalk or pencil. Machine stitch all round the outline, then cut round the shape 1cm (³⁄₈in) outside the line of stitching.

12 Turn back the allowance beyond the stitched line, so that the stitching cannot be seen from the front. Snip where necessary, so that the turnings lie flat. Press.

13 Pin the urn in position on the cushion front and slip stitch to the cushion using tiny stitches. Remove the pins.

14 Work all round the outline of the urn in stem stitch using three strands of gold thread.

ROSEBUD

Ribbon stitch

Side ribbon stitch

PEONY

Lazy daisy stitch

Ribbon stitch

Pistil stitch

LILAC

● ◎   French knot

ROSE

        Lazy daisy stitch

        Side ribbon stitch

        Ribbon stitch

MUSTARD FLOWER

●   French knot

        Coral stitch

TURQUOISE FLOWER

●   French knot

        French knot

FOLIAGE BRANCHES

        Ribbon stitch

        Side ribbon stitch

        Stem stitch

        Lazy daisy stitch

        Fly stitch and

        Straight stitch

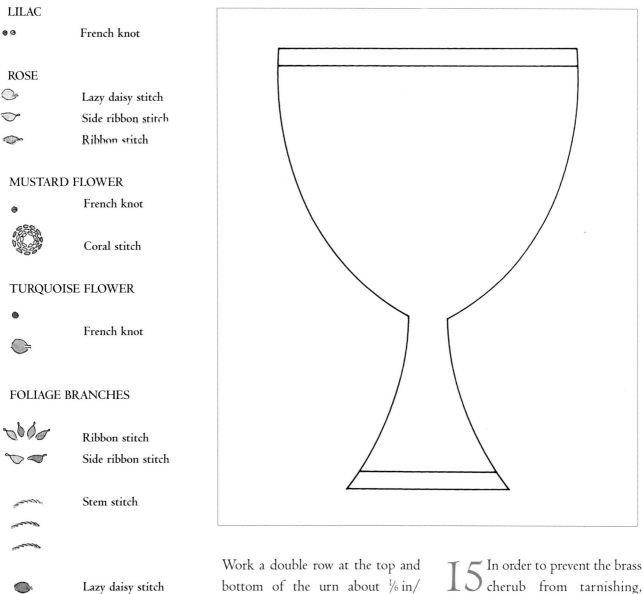

Work a double row at the top and bottom of the urn about ⅙ in/ 4mm apart. Fill in the space between these two rows with diagonal straight stitches.

15 In order to prevent the brass cherub from tarnishing, wash it in soapy water, dry, then seal the surface with a clear varnish. Stick the cherub in position on the urn using fabric glue. A hot glue gun

PILLOWCASE & SHEET

I have always loved beautiful bed linen. This book provided the opportunity for me to design some linen that would be wonderful to use when guests come to stay. The materials given will embroider a single bed set.

YOU WILL NEED

1²/₃yd/1.5m 4mm dark pink
   silk ribbon
40in/1m 4mm medium pink
   silk ribbon
2³/₄yd/2.5m 4mm light pink
   silk ribbon
1²/₃yd/1.5m 7mm medium
   pink silk ribbon
Variegated green pearl cotton
40in/1m 7mm light green
   silk ribbon
2½yd/2.3m pink Mokuba
   ribbon
Pink embroidery floss (to match
   Mokuba ribbon)
Tailor's chalk or dressmaker's
   marking pencil
Storebought pillowcase and single
   sheet
Embroidery hoop or frame
No. 18 chenille needle
Crewel or similar needle

To stitch the pillowcase

1 Since you will want to launder the embroidered bed linen, soak the ribbons in cold, salted water before using. This will prevent the dye from running in any subsequent washes.

2 Draw the design onto the top left-hand corner of the pillowcase following the stem shapes shown in the stitch diagram on page 52 and using tailor's chalk or pencil. Stretch this area on an embroidery hoop or frame.

3 Using the three shades of 4mm pink ribbon, work the three bullion roses in the positions shown in the stitch diagram.

4 Next work the outer petals of the bullion roses in ribbon stitch using the 7mm medium pink ribbon.

5 Using the same color, work the large buds in ribbon stitch and side ribbon stitch.

6 Work two sprays of buds in light pink in ribbon stitch and one in dark pink.

7 Next, with a pin, mark the place where the bow will cross the stems. This will give you a point at which to bring the stems together. Then stitch the eight stems in stem stitch, using the variegated green pearl cotton.

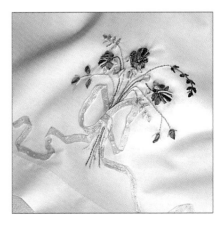

8 Using the same pearl cotton to match the stems, work around the buds in fly stitch with a straight stitch from the base of the bud to the center on some of the buds.

9 With the 7mm light green ribbon, work the leaves around the flowers of the bullion roses and down the stem in both ribbon stitch and side ribbon stitch.

10 Using the Mokuba ribbon, bring the needle up through the pillowcase at a point approximately 4½in/10.5m below the lowest left-hand flower bud. Then lay the ribbon in a bow on the pillowcase, crossing the stems at their narrowest point. Add twists and turns into the long tails and pin in place. Then take the ribbon to the back of the case approximately 4½in/10.5m to the right of the farthest right-hand large bud.

11 Finish off carefully at the back. Attach the ribbon to the fabric along its length with French knots made using two strands of matching embroidery floss and spacing them about ⅜in/1cm apart.

To stitch the sheet

Work the design onto the sheet in the same way with only one difference: the bow tails will now take different twists and turns. Position the design just below the top large hem in the center. The bow is nearest to the hem with the flowers pointing away from it so that the design will be the right way up when the linen is on the bed.

	Fly stitch and straight stitch
	Bullion stitch
	Ribbon stitch
	Stem stitch
	French knot

PELMET & TIEBACKS

Damask is an ideal fabric for curtains and perfectly suitable for silk ribbon embroidery. For this design I wanted to add just a little color to reflect the colors and style of the room. The abstract design evolved from the triangular design of the pelmet and tiebacks and is loosely reminiscent of a jester juggling. This pelmet fits flush into a recess. It's a simple project, highly suitable for a beginner, utilizing just three stitches in a straightforward combination.

YOU WILL NEED

Stiffened stick-on pelmet backing (See method.)
Damask fabric or your own choice (See method.)
Embroidery hoop or frame
No. 18 chenille needle
Approximately 2¼yd/2.3m 7mm Mokuba variegated sylk ribbon color 001
Approximately 40in/1m 3.5mm Mokuba variegated silk ribbon color 001
Fabric glue and brush
Storebought tassels (one for each point of the pelmet)
Sewing thread
4 curtain rings

To stitch the pelmet

1 The number of triangles required depends on the length of your pelmet. Measure your window frame and divide by 9½in/24cm to find the number you will need. One of these will be made up of two half-triangles (for each end of the pelmet). If the required width does not divide exactly, you can adjust the number of triangles and/or the length of the overlap (see Diagram 1, page 57). If the amount left over is more than 5in/13cm, add an extra triangle and increase the length of the overlap. If it is under 5in/13cm, just reduce the length of the overlap.

2 Make a pattern for the triangles from the template on page 54, measuring 14in/36cm across and 14in/36cm long.

3 Cut the required number of triangles out of stiffened pelmet fabric. Cut one in half through the vertical center line. Cut the same number of fabric triangles but allow an additional ⅝in/1.5cm seam allowance all around.

4 Starting 5¼in/13.6cm up from the bottom point of the first full triangle for the pelmet, mark the center of the fabric with a pin. Stretch the fabric on an embroidery hoop or frame.

5 Using the 7mm width variegated ribbon, work three ribbon stitches each ¾in/2cm long radiating out from the point marked by the pin as shown in the closeup photograph on page 56. Next, work a short horizontal straight stitch directly under the three previously worked stitches.

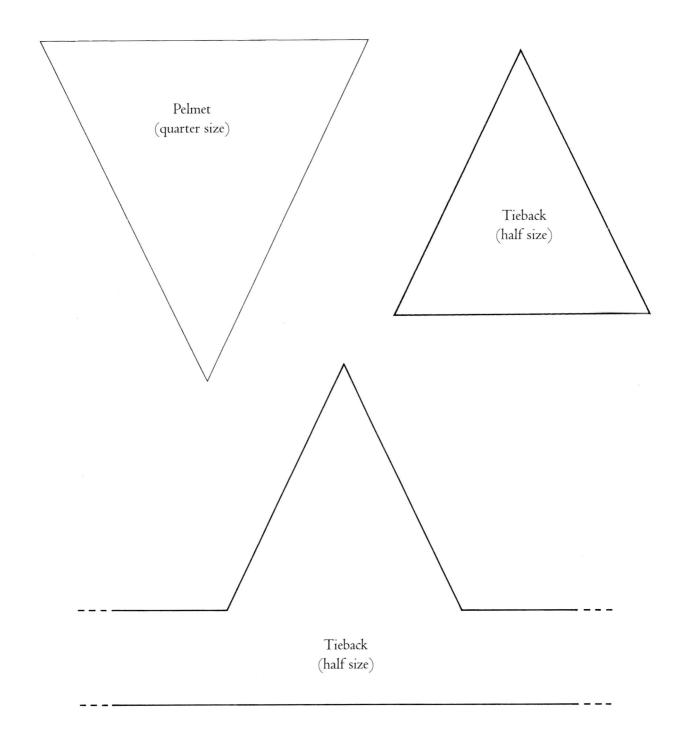

Pelmet
(quarter size)

Tieback
(half size)

Tieback
(half size)

6 Work a French knot directly underneath, then a French knot at the tip of the two side stitches and two above the middle stitch. Repeat in the same position on the point of each full triangle.

7 On the half-triangles at each end of the pelmet, work the center ribbon stitch in 3.5mm wide ribbon and just one ribbon stitch either to the left or to the right depending on whether this is the left- or right-hand half-triangle.

NOTES AND TIPS

The secret with this design is to be selective about the lengths of ribbon cut from the variegated reel, so that you work the right colors in the appropriate places.

To stitch the tiebacks

1 Measure the length of tieback required by placing a tape measure around the curtain at the required height and to the required fullness. Cut out a piece of stiffened

pelmet backing to this length and 2in/5cm wide with a triangle point in the center, following the template. Cut a triangle, using the tieback template. Cut the same shapes in fabric, two of each, adding seam allowances as before.

2 Work the tiebacks in exactly the same way as the pelmet but with the 3.5mm width ribbon throughout. The base of the ribbon stitch is 4¼in/11cm up from the point on the large triangle and 3½in/9cm up on the small one.

To make the pelmet

1 Place one of the pelmet backing triangles centrally on the reverse of the embroidered triangle and press firmly.

2 Fold back the seam allowance of the fabric and press down, folding in the corner of the point neatly. Use a little glue to hold the fabric down, or secure it with a few stitches if necessary. Repeat with the other triangles.

3 Lay out the triangles in a row, with a half-triangle at each end.

Every alternate triangle is placed behind the ones on either side, starting with the half-triangles underneath so that there is an 4½in/11cm overlap (see Diagram I). Mark the points of the overlaps with pins, apply glue to the overlapping area on the underneath triangles, then stick down.

4 Stick or stitch tassels to the point of each triangle.

5 Cut a piece of pelmet backing to the exact length of the pelmet and 4in/10cm deep. Lay the length of embroidered triangles on top. Press until firmly stuck.

6 Fix a pelmet board to the window. Apply glue to the

14in/36cm 9½in/24cm 4½in/
11cm

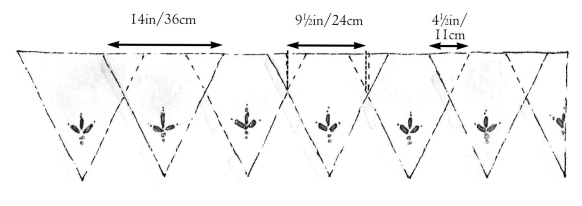

Diagram 1

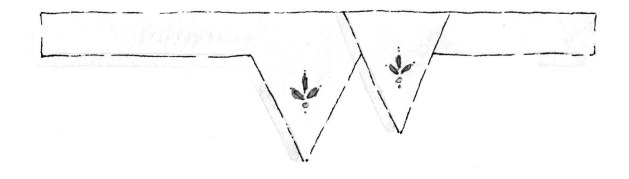

Diagram 2

uppermost side of the board and press the pelmet in position.

To make the tiebacks

1 Stick the stiffened pelmet backing to the fabric for the tieback and for the triangles, folding the fabric to the back in the same way as for the pelmet. Stick one triangle to each tieback as shown in Diagram 2.

2 Stitch curtain rings to the back of the tieback at each end. Fix wall hooks at the desired height.

TABLECLOTH & NAPKINS

Summer afternoon teas look wonderful when served on fresh crisp table linen. I have worked a bold abstract design on a lovely lemon yellow cotton chintz for this project. The tablecloth would also look very pretty as the overcloth on a round occasional table, picking up the color from a print floor-length cloth underneath. This quantity of fabric is enough for the cloth and two napkins.

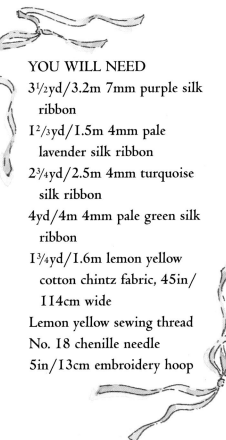

YOU WILL NEED
3½yd/3.2m 7mm purple silk ribbon

1⅔yd/1.5m 4mm pale lavender silk ribbon

2¾yd/2.5m 4mm turquoise silk ribbon

4yd/4m 4mm pale green silk ribbon

1¾yd/1.6m lemon yellow cotton chintz fabric, 45in/ 114cm wide

Lemon yellow sewing thread

No. 18 chenille needle

5in/13cm embroidery hoop

To stitch and make the design

1 Since you will want to launder the table linen, soak the ribbon in cold, salted water before using. This will prevent the dye from running in any subsequent washes.

2 Cut one square 45in/114cm wide for the tablecloth and two 17½in/45cm squares for the napkins from the remainder.

3 Turn under a narrow hem ⅜in/1cm wide on the large square and press, then turn under the same amount again and press to create a double hem. Machine stitch in place. Repeat on both the squares for the napkins.

4 Work the design shown in the photograph on page 60 in all four corners of the tablecloth and one corner on each napkin as follows: Stretch one corner of the fabric onto the hoop; there should be a border of approximately 1in/2.5cm overhanging the hoop. Using the purple ribbon, work one large lazy daisy stitch in the center of the stretched fabric.

5 Taking the same ribbon, work three or four long twisted straight stitches. To do this, twist the ribbon after you have pulled it through to the front, then take the needle to the back of the fabric, leaving a loose stitch at the front. The end of the stitch will form a spiral curl, and the way the ribbon curls will determine whether you have space for three or four stitches.

6 Changing to the pale lavender ribbon, work three more long, twisted, straight stitches. Now with

the turquoise ribbon, work three more long, twisted, straight stitches.

7 Still using the turquoise ribbon, work approximately five or six loop stitches in the middle of the shape.

8 Using the green ribbon, add five twisted ribbon stitch leaves to the bottom of the design. Work the stitch as described on page 17, but put a single twist in the ribbon.

9 Still using the green ribbon, work lazy daisy leaves around the bottom of the design as shown.

NOTES AND TIPS

Twist the ribbon many times to get it to curl, but do not twist too tightly or the fronds will be too thin.

Muslin Hat

I spotted this delightful hat at a craft fair and instantly fell in love with it. The hat lent itself to my design, which can be worked in any combination of colors. Perhaps you would like to work it in primary colors, mixing and matching the loop colors with the knot colors?

YOU WILL NEED
Store-bought hat
5in/13cm embroidery hoop
No. 18 chenille needle
3½yd/3.2m ⅛in/3mm tan silk
  ribbon
3½yd/3.2m 3mm black
  silk ribbon

To stitch the design

1 If the hat is lined, as mine was, you will need to unpick the crown lining before you start so that the back of the work will not be exposed on the inside of the hat.

2 Using the embroidery hoop, stretch a section of the hat. (I started at the center back and worked to the left.)

3 This simple stitch is a kind of crossed lazy daisy anchored by a French knot. Starting with the tan ribbon, work the stitch as shown in the diagram below, bringing the needle up at A and down at B, then up again at C and down at D. The stitch is about ½in/13mm high.

4 Place a pin through the ribbon at the point where it crosses over (E). Change to the black ribbon, bring the needle up at E, and work a French knot.

5 Work a second pattern stitch in the same way as the first, leaving about ¼in/6mm between the two stitches.

6 Change the colors so that the crossed lazy daisy is worked in black and the French knot in tan. Work two stitches, then change back to the original colors.

7 Change the color combination every two pattern stitches.

8 Work all around the hat, moving the embroidery hoop along as you progress. Continue until you meet up with the first stitch.

9 When you have finished your embroidery, slip stitch the lining back into place in the crown of the hat.

VARIATION

You could easily work this design on a ribbon to make a hatband as in the following project. Use a grosgrain ribbon or even an edged strip of fabric.

Other applications for this design might be for the collar of a blouse or on the edge of a pocket.

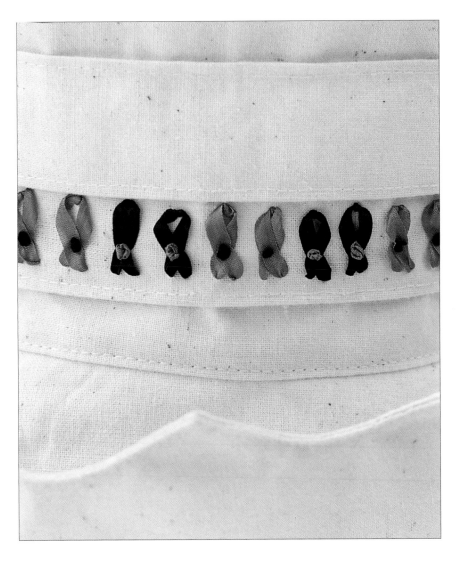

 NOTES AND TIPS

After every four or five stitches, it is a good idea to measure the last stitch to make sure you're keeping to the correct size, rather than gradually scaling up or down.

Sunflower Hatband

Sunflowers are always popular. They have a simple, summery look about them, which makes them a perfect design to decorate a straw hat. This embroidery is worked on double wire-edged ribbon, which is easily tied into a flamboyant bow. The design is made up of fully open sunflowers and buds in varying positions.
Some have stems, some don't: it's up to you.

YOU WILL NEED

1²⁄₃yd/1.5m green double
 wire-edged silk ribbon,
 1¹⁄₂in/4cm wide
Store-bought straw hat
5in/13mm embroidery hoop
No. 18 chenille needle
Crewel or similar needle
1¹⁄₂yd/1.3m 4mm brown silk
 ribbon
1²⁄₃yd/1.5m 4mm orange silk
 ribbon
3yd/2.7m 7mm yellow silk
 ribbon
40in/1m 13mm green silk
 ribbon
20in/51cm 7mm green silk
 ribbon
Matching green embroidery
 floss

To stitch the design

1 Tie the wire-edged ribbon around the hat, making a full bow at one side. Trim the ends into a V shape. With pins mark the center front and back of the hat on the ribbon.

2 Leaving the ribbon tied in a bow, carefully remove it from the hat and stretch it on the embroidery hoop. Start stitching at the pin; mark the center front and work your first whole sunflower in the middle of the band as described in the following steps.

3 With brown ribbon, work one French knot surrounded by a circle of French knots. Change to orange ribbon and work a second circle of French knots. Using the yellow ribbon, work petals in ribbon stitch all around the circle of French knots.

4 Using the 13mm green ribbon, work leaves in ribbon stitch randomly below the flower head. You could also add some smaller leaves using the 7mm green ribbon. Stitch the stem with two strands of embroidery floss and work in stem stitch.

5 Work a half-open bud on either side as follows: Stitch a central French knot in brown with three or four others in a half-circle close to it. Add a second half-circle in orange, then five or six ribbon stitch petals radiating out from the French knots. Add a leaf in 13mm green ribbon and a stem as before.

6 Work a closed bud to the left of the flowers already stitched as follows: Using yellow ribbon, work two back-to-back ribbon stitches, then a straight stitch in green ribbon underneath; below that, one or two ribbon stitch leaves in 13mm green ribbon and a stem as before.

7 The stitch diagram below shows the three variations described above in a suggested arrangement. Follow this until your wire-edged ribbon is full, or just work your own pattern of flowers.

⬭	Ribbon stitch
•	French knot
﹏	Stem stitch
⬬	Straight stitch

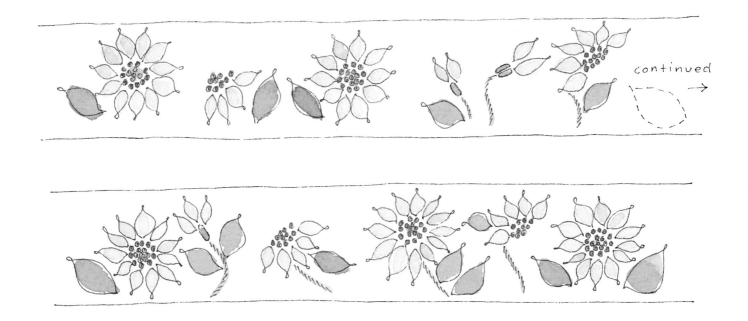

continued →

CHINESE LINEN BLOUSE

For this Chinese-style blouse, I've chosen a classic design, one that never goes out of fashion. The blouse provided me with the motif, which is reminiscent of the blue-and-white willow pattern on china. Even a small amount of embroidery will personalize a store-bought blouse. Because the design I have used is not too fussy, the blouse can be worn with jeans or dressed up to wear in the evening.

YOU WILL NEED

20in/51cm 4mm medium blue silk ribbon
20in/51cm 4mm light blue silk ribbon
10in/25cm 7mm dusty blue silk ribbon
Dark gray embroidery floss
10in/25cm 4mm very dark blue/purple silk ribbon
10in/25cm 4mm dark blue silk ribbon
Store-bought blouse
Tailor's chalk or dressmaker's marking pencil
5in/13cm embroidery hoop
No. 18 chenille needle
Crewel or similar needle

To stitch the design

1 Since you will want to launder the embroidery, soak the ribbon in cold, salted water before using. This will prevent the dye from running in any subsequent washes.

2 Mark the position of the bird and the flower onto the blouse with tailor's chalk or pencil, following the outline of the full-size stitch diagram below.

3 Stretch the area to be worked onto the embroidery hoop.

- Straight stitch (ribbon)
- French knot
- Ribbon stitch
- Side ribbon stitch
- Stem stitch
- Straight stitch (floss)

4 Following the ribbon colors in the diagram, work the main left-hand part of the wing first with a single straight stitch, then the small feathers up the right-hand side of the wing also in straight stitch, varying their length and fanning them out toward the top.

5 Next, stitch the body, then the tail feathers and the head, all in straight stitch.

6 Using two strands of the embroidery floss, work a straight stitch for the beak and a French knot for the eye.

7 Work the flower by starting with two small straight stitches in the very dark blue/purple ribbon, then work four petals in the 7mm dusty blue ribbon; use ribbon stitch: the two outermost petals give the flower head a better shape if they are worked in side ribbon stitch.

8 Work three petals in between the four just worked in ribbon stitch, using the dark blue ribbon.

9 To finish, change to two strands of the embroidery floss and work the stem in stem stitch, then the stamen in straight stitch.

NOTES AND TIPS

Since no two people are the same shape or size, it is a good idea to try the blouse on in order to mark the best position for the embroidery. The design could also be worked on a vest or jacket.

EVENING WRAP

I had the idea that I wanted to produce a very luxurious evening wrap. Not an everyday useful item, but an item that in years to come will be found in a drawer and mused upon. A "what was it worn for and by whom" garment. The ribbon colors blend with the silk fabric, creating a rich but subtle decoration at either end of the wrap.

YOU WILL NEED

1yd/1m metallic shot silk fabric

2yd/1.8m lining fabric

Matching sewing thread for beads and fabric

8in/20cm embroidery hoop or frame

No. 18 chenille needle

2¼yd/2m Mokuba 7mm luminous moss green ribbon

Sewing thread to match moss green Mokuba

6½yd/6m Mokuba 7mm raysheen dark green ribbon

6½yd/6m Mokuba 9mm metallic green organdy ribbon

1 2.25g packet glass beads

Beading needle

To stitch the design

1 Cut the metallic silk fabric in half lengthwise, then machine stitch the two pieces together to make one long scarf shape. Trim and neaten the seam edges.

2 Cut the lining in two crosswise, then cut and join each piece as for the metallic silk to make two lengths of lining.

3 Place the metallic silk on top of one of the lining pieces, with wrong sides together. Machine-stitch the two layers together around all four sides ½in/13mm away from the edge. You are now going to treat the two fabrics as one and embroider through both. The lining gives stability to the silk.

4 With a pin, mark the center of the width of the silk fabric

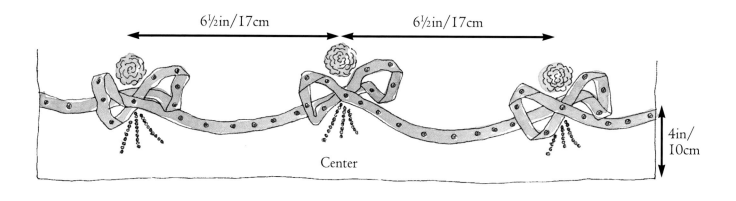

6½in/17cm   6½in/17cm

Center

4in/
10cm

⊛ Pre-gathered rose

• French knot

⚬⚬⚬ Beads

4in/10cm from one short edge. Stretch this area of the fabric on a hoop or frame.

5 Using the luminous ribbon, work three pre-gathered roses and stitch them onto the fabric as shown in the diagram above.

6 Change to the raysheen ribbon and lay it onto the fabric as shown. Pin into position, taking the ends of this ribbon beyond the machine-stitched line.

7 Using the organdy ribbon, work French knots at regular intervals to secure the raysheen ribbon to the fabric, removing the pins as you go.

8 With the beading needle, stitch the beads onto the fabric to make three tails under each bow. There are approximately 12 beads in each tail.

9 Repeat Steps 4 to 8 at the other end of the wrap.

To make the wrap

1 Take the second piece of the lining fabric and place it on top of the embroidered pieces, right sides together. Stitch all around the sides of the wrap, trapping the ends of the raysheen ribbon as you do so. Take a ⅝ in/1.5cm seam allowance and leave a short 6in/15cm gap on one long side.

2 Turn the wrap right side out through the gap, then hand-stitch the sides of the gap together.

NOTES AND TIPS

Try to space the French knots at an equal distance apart along the raysheen ribbon. Stitch each of the bead tails in a slightly different direction and to varying lengths to add interest to the design.

EVENING VEST

I have yearned for some time to design some elegant evening wear. This attractive vest and the wrap on page 71 are the result. The vest is very simple to work, using only one basic silk ribbon stitch. You could work this design on any store-bought or homemade waistcoat. As with the wrap, the ribbon colors blend with the silk fabric to produce a rich but understated garment.

YOU WILL NEED

Blue-green shot dupioni silk (amount according to pattern instructions)

Tailor's chalk or dressmaker's marking pencil

5in/13mm embroidery hoop

No. 18 chenille needle

Crewel or similar needle

1 skein blue-green embroidery floss

1 skein jade green embroidery floss to match ribbon

11yd/10m 4mm jade green silk ribbon

1 2.25g packet emerald green seed beads

Beading needle

Sewing thread to match beads

To stitch and make the design

1 If you are making the vest yourself, lay the pattern pieces on the fabric and either draw or baste around the shapes.

2 With the full-size stitch diagram on page 74, draw the design of the stalks and branches on the fabric shape for the right-hand vest front; use either a pencil or tailor's chalk. Take the design to the shoulder of your vest and end the central stem with a curl. Note that the stalks are just curved lines and the branches for the berries are somewhat curlier at the ends. Be careful to avoid button or buttonhole placements.

3 Stretch the lower area of the design on the embroidery hoop. Note that you do not cut any of the fabric pieces until all the embroidery is completed. This is to make it easier to fit the narrow fronts on the hoop and to prevent fraying.

4 Using two strands of the blue-green embroidery floss, work the center stalk of the design up the front of the vest in stem stitch.

5 Work all the side stems; use one strand of the jade green embroidery floss and work in stem stitch again.

6 With the silk ribbon, work pairs of leaves on the side stems (follow the stitch diagram for position) in ribbon and side ribbon stitch as appropriate (see pages 17 and 18).

7 Take the seed beads and use the beading needle to stitch them

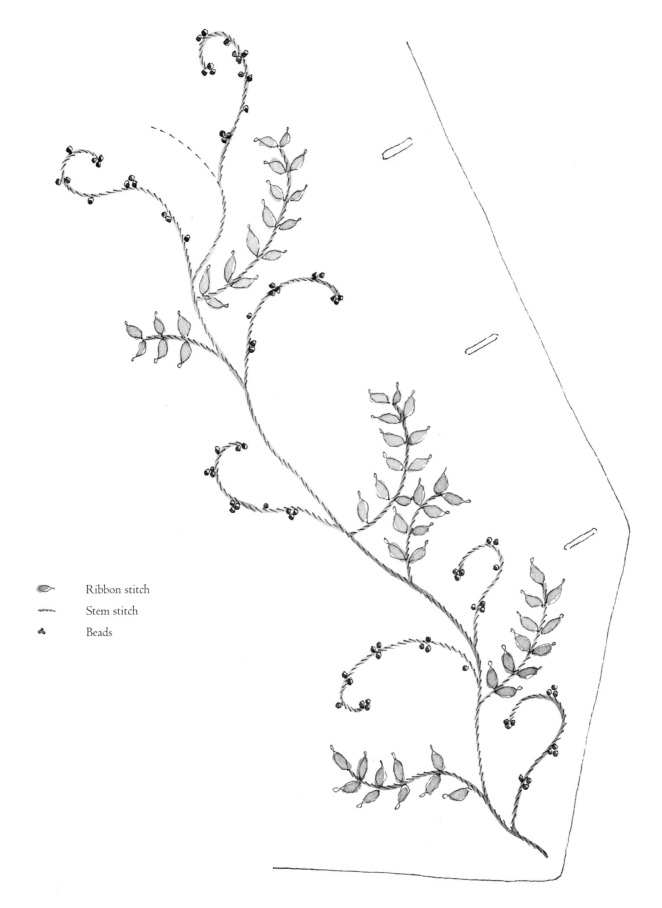

Ribbon stitch

Stem stitch

Beads

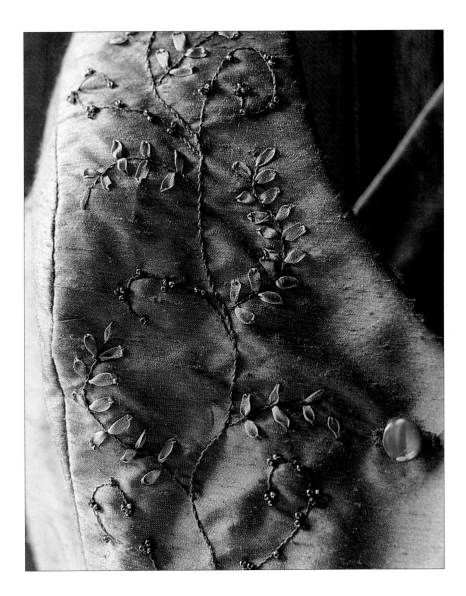

NOTES AND TIPS

I used only a small embroidery hoop, moving it up as I completed each segment of the design. That is easier than trying to stretch all the fabric for the whole design. Try to make both sides of the vest identical, or at least balanced.

If you work this design on a store-bought vest, remember to unpick the lining first so that the back of the embroidery will be between the two layers.

onto the remaining stems either singly or in clusters of two or three.

8 Work the pattern in the same way on the left-hand front but make the design a mirror image.

Cut out all the pattern pieces and make up the vest according to the pattern instructions.

GIFT BOX

This is a simple little design set onto the lid of a fabric-covered box. The box makes a gift in itself, but it could also be used to hold a special memento from an important occasion, such as a wedding or a christening.

YOU WILL NEED

I piece of cream silk, 10 x 10in/
25 x 25cm, for the lid inset
Tailor's chalk or dressmaker's
marking pencil
5in/13cm embroidery hoop
No. 18 chenille needle
Crewel or similar needle
40in/1m 7mm pale green silk
ribbon
Pale pink embroidery floss to
blend with the pink ribbon
20in/51cm 4mm pale lemon
silk ribbon
20in/51cm 4mm pale pink silk
ribbon
Green embroidery floss to blend
with the green ribbon
Cardboard or template plastic
Sharp craft knife
Stiff cardboard approximately
⅛in/3mm thick
I piece of felt, 17 x 10in/
43 x 25cm

Piece of lemon yellow silk,
18 x 12in/46 x 30cm, for
the outside of the box
Fabric glue and narrow glue
brush
Lemon yellow sewing thread
Curved needle
Piece of lining (I used cream
silk) 24 x 12in/61 x 30cm
Circle of batting, 3in/8cm
in diameter
12in/30cm pearl beading or
narrow decorative cord

To stitch the design

1 Mark a circle approximately
3in/8cm in diameter in the center of the piece of cream silk fabric for the lid inset with chalk or pencil. Stretch the fabric on the embroidery hoop.

2 Following the stitch diagram on page 78 and using green silk ribbon, start in the center of the circle and work a Merrilyn bow. Do not take the bow nearer than ⅜in/1cm to the edge of the circle. Twist the tails to add interest.

3 Using two strands of pink embroidery floss, work two spider webs ¾in/2cm up from the bow and ¼in/6mm apart. Change to the lemon ribbon and work two rounds of the roses, then finish the roses in pale pink ribbon.

4 Work two ribbon stitch buds in pink ribbon, as on the stitch diagram. Then with two strands of green embroidery floss, work the leaves in fly stitch, with a straight stitch into the center of the bud.

5 Using green ribbon, work four ribbon stitch leaves around the spider web roses.

To make the box

1 Using the sharp craft knife, cut out the six templates A to F on page 81 in cardboard or plastic. Use the templates to cut the specified number of pieces from the stiff card-

🎀 Merrilyn bow

🌀 Spider web rose

🌱 Fly stitch and straight stitch

〜 Ribbon stitch

board and number them, as follows:
4 from template A (Nos. 1, 2, 3, 4)
2 from template B (Nos. 6 and 7)
2 from template C (Nos. 5 and 11)
2 from template D (Nos. 8 and 9)
1 from template E (No. 10)
2 from template F (Nos. 12 and 13)
Cut out the inner circle from one of the pieces cut from template F (piece No. 12).

2 Score the right-hand side of pieces 1 to 4 along the dotted line shown on template A. Spread a thin layer of glue on the unscored side of these pieces, then lay them,

glue side down, side by side on the felt. Trim the felt to fit the outside of the shapes. This makes a unit that will form the sides of the box. Glue felt to all the other pieces separately except for No. 13.

3 Place the lemon yellow silk fabric, right side down, on the work surface. Then place the sides of the box on top, felt side down, and trim the silk to within ⅝in/1.5cm of the sides (see Diagram 1 on page 82). Do the same with No. 5 (the bottom of the box).

4 Brush a thin line of glue around the edges of the unfelted side for both the sides and the bottom of the box. Working on the unit for the sides of the box first, fold over the two short sides of the silk onto the cardboard and press evenly to stick them down. Fold in the corners, then fold over and stick the two long sides. Repeat for the bottom of the box.

5 Form the unit for the sides of the box into a box shape by bringing the two short sides together, with the lemon silk on the outside. Using sewing thread and

the curved needle, ladder-stitch the two short sides together (See diagram 2 on page 82). Place the bottom of the box in position, again with the lemon silk on the outside and stitch in place. This makes the base of the box.

6 Nos. 6 to 10 are the inside and base lining pieces, and No. 11 is the lid lining. Glue pieces of cream lining silk to each of these separately in the same way as for piece No. 5.

7 Brush a thin layer of glue over the unfelted side of pieces 6 and 7, then position them opposite each other on the inside of the box. Glue pieces 8 and 9 in the same way and press inside the box on the two remaining sides. Glue piece 10 and press it into the base of the box.

8 Lay piece No. 12 on the wrong side of the lemon yellow fabric, felt side down, and cut round the silk allowing 1½in/4cm extra all around each side of the cardboard.

9 Hold the cardboard and silk firmly in one hand, then pierce the middle of the circular hole with

a pair of sharp embroidery scissors. Cut out carefully almost to the edges of the circle. Repeat all around the circle, working out in segments (see Diagram 3 on page 82). Glue around the outside of the circle; fold back the segments of fabric and stick them firmly down.

10 Glue lightly around the edge of the circle. Place the embroidered piece of cream silk, right side up, on a work surface and very carefully position piece 12 over it so that the embroidery shows centrally in the circular opening. Press it in place; pull the edges gently to ensure that the embroidered fabric is taut, then turn it over. Trim the excess cream silk, then lay the small piece of batting centrally over the embroidery.

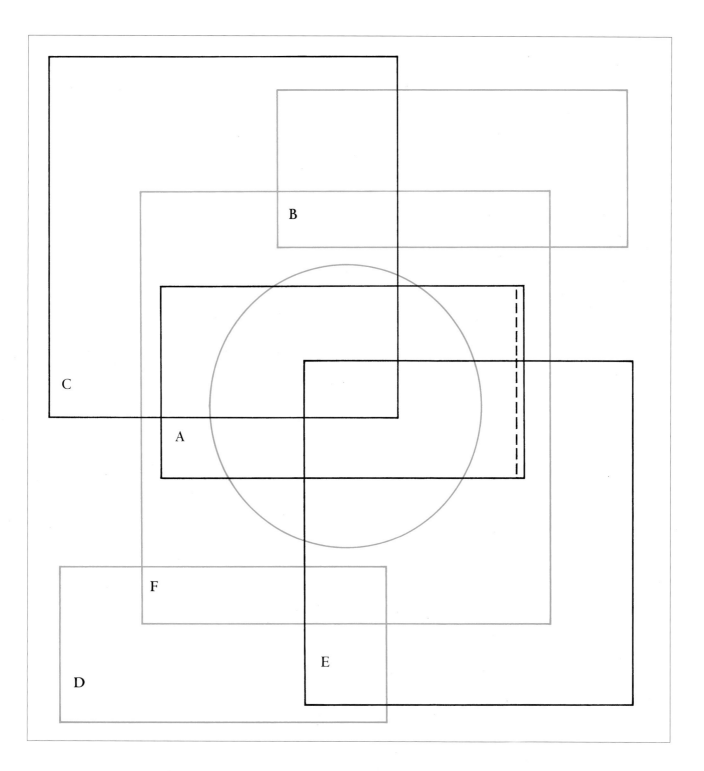

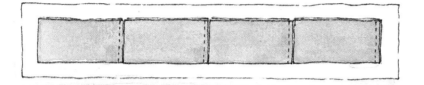

Diagram 1

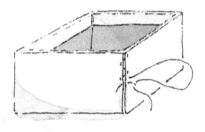

Diagram 2

Diagram 3

piece 11 and press down centrally on the underside of the lid (see Diagram 4).

13 Spread glue very lightly on the pearl beading and position it around the outside of the circle on the top of the lid to finish.

NOTES AND TIPS

If you are going to make more than one box (there are two different designs in this book), it is worth cutting the templates from plastic so that they can be used more than once.

Handle the silk carefully once you have cut around the edge of the inner circle; it frays very easily.

Diagram 4

11 Place piece No. 13 on top. Glue a 1½in/4cm strip around the sides of the back of the lid. Fold back and stick down the silk turnings. Work on two opposite sides first, neaten the corners, then fold back the two remaining sides.

12 Spread a thin layer of glue on the uncovered side of

PADDED PICTURE FRAME

This picture frame can be used as a gift for many different occasions. For a wedding or christening photograph, a nice touch is to make it out of the same fabric as the dress worn by the bride or baby for the actual occasion. I used silk dupioni, an inexpensive but luxurious fabric with a lovely surface texture. The outside measurement of the frame is 12 x 10in/30 x 25cm and the aperture 6½ x 5in/17 x 13cm but you could adjust the size to fit your own requirements.

YOU WILL NEED

40in/1m 9mm cream double-edged satin ribbon

40in/1m 9mm medium pink double-edged satin ribbon

40in/1m 9mm dark pink double-edged satin ribbon

20in/51cm silk fabric, 45in/114cm wide

Embroidery hoop or frame

No. 18 chenille needle

Crewel or similar needle

Tailor's chalk or dressmaker's marking pencil

20in/51cm 4mm off-white silk ribbon

Pink sewing thread to match satin ribbons

1 length light lemon embroidery floss

1 length light pink embroidery floss

40in/1m gold embroidery thread

Gold colored sewing thread

40in/1m ¾in/20mm wide 10in wire-edged gold ribbon

Bow maker (optional)

2 pieces stiff cardboard, 12 x 10in/30 x 25cm each

1 piece lightweight batting, 12 x 10in/30 x 25cm

Fabric glue

2 small adhesive hooks and hanging cord (optional)

1 piece stiff cardboard, 2½ x 10in/ 6 x 25cm for a stand (optional)

To stitch the design

1 Make three cream, two medium pink and three dark pink double-edged satin roses with the satin ribbons.

2 Cut a piece of fabric 14 x 16in/36 x 41 cm for the front of the frame. Mark the center top of the fabric. Stretch on an embroidery hoop or frame. Stitch the roses onto the fabric, as shown in the stitch diagram on page 84.

3 Using the off-white silk ribbon, work 11 French knots in the positions shown.

4 Using two strands of the light lemon embroidery floss, stitch clusters of three French knots in the positions shown.

5 Using two strands of the light pink embroidery floss, work straight stitches radiating out from the lemon French knots.

6 Using all six strands of the gold thread and working in stem stitch, stitch the rope on either side of the flowers in the shape shown. (It's a good idea to draw it on first with chalk or pencil.)

7 Make two small bows without tails in the gold wire-edged ribbon. (You could use someone else's fingers to get the size right, but if you have a bow maker that would be ideal.) Stitch down the ribbon ends with the sewing thread, then stitch onto the silk as shown.

To make the frame

I Cut a rectangle 6 ½ x 5in/17 x 13cm from the middle of one of the pieces of cardboard; leave a 2¾in/7cm border at top and bottom and 2½in/6cm at the sides. Cover the front of the frame with batting and glue it down.

Double-edged satin rose

French knot

Straight stitch

Stem stitch

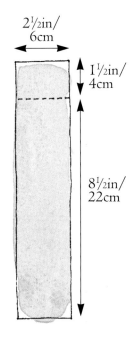

2½in/
6cm

1½in/
4cm

8½in/
22cm

2 Spread a little glue over the batting. Lay the embroidered fabric centrally over the frame front, right side up, and gently press it into position.

3 Pierce the middle of the fabric covering the aperture with a pair of sharp embroidery scissors and cut diagonally out to each corner of the frame to within ¼in/6mm of the corner. Put a small spot of glue at each corner to prevent fraying. Trim off the points. Glue the edges of the sides of the aperture at the back and fold the fabric back onto it.

4 Fold the fabric around the outer edges of the frame front to the back and glue down. Make small cuts around the edges to allow the fabric to stick to the back of the cardboard without puckering, and miter the corners carefully.

5 Cut a second piece of fabric 12 x 14in/30 x 36cm to cover the front of the second piece of cardboard (the back board), glue and stick, turning the excess to the back.

6 Cut a third piece to the same dimensions. Turn under a 1in/2.5cm hem and machine stitch all around. Glue this piece to the reverse of the back board.

7 Place the two boards wrong sides together and, with a curved needle, ladder-stitch the top and two sides together, leaving the bottom open to insert a photo.

8 If you wish to hang your frame on the wall, you can buy small self-adhesive hooks. But if you wish it to stand, then you need to cut a third piece of cardboard in the shape shown in diagram at right above. Score along the dotted line to make a hinge. Cover it in fabric cut ½in/1.5cm bigger than the cardboard to wrap around the edges. Cut another piece of fabric to cover the back of the stand below the hinge and glue it in place. Glue the area above the hinge very firmly to the center back of the frame so

that the bottom is level with the bottom of the frame.

NOTES AND TIPS

If you are working with silk or any fabric that tends to fray easily, you can stick a length of pearl beading around the inside edge in order to hide any of the little cuts that may show on the front of the work. (They do tend to run when you are pulling the fabric firm over the cardboard frame.)

CHRISTENING GOWN

I have worked ribbon embroidery onto a number of christening gowns. It looks fabulous. I usually work in the same color as the fabric (white or cream), but for the photograph—so that you can see the design better—I have used ice cream-colored ribbons. I have made up this little dress in silk dupioni with a lace edging on the skirt and the cuffs, and ribbon bows at the sleeves. Any store-bought or homemade dress is suitable provided it has a plain yoke like the one shown here.

YOU WILL NEED
Store-bought christening gown
or
Silk fabric to make one (amount
   as pattern instructions)
Tailor's chalk or dressmaker's
   marking pencil
Embroidery hoop or frame
No. 18 chenille needle
Crewel or similar needle
1²⁄₃ yd/1.5m 7mm pale pink
   silk ribbon
4³⁄₄ yd/4.3m 4mm pale lemon
   silk ribbon
20in/51cm 7mm pale green
   silk ribbon
Ivory embroidery floss
1 2–3g packet seed pearl beads
Beading needle
Sewing thread to match
   beads and ribbons

To stitch and make the design

1 If you are making the dress yourself, lay the pattern pieces on the fabric and either draw or baste around the shapes.

2 Mark the center of the front yoke. Stretch this area on an embroidery hoop or frame. To minimize fraying, do not cut the pattern pieces until all the embroidery is completed.

3 Using the pink and the lemon ribbons, work a pre-gathered rose and stitch it in the center spot of the yoke. Work two more roses and stitch them on either side of the center rose, each 1¹⁄₂ in/4cm away from it.

4 With the lemon ribbon, work two five-petal flowers in ribbon stitch, each one centrally between and below the pre-gathered roses (see stitch diagram on page 88).

5 Use the green ribbon to work three ribbon stitch leaves above the roses positioned as shown in the diagram.

6 Utilize two strands of the embroidery floss to stitch four lazy daisy flowers in the positions shown.

Merrilyn bow	
Pre-gathered rose	
Lazy daisy stitch	
Ribbon stitch	
Bead	

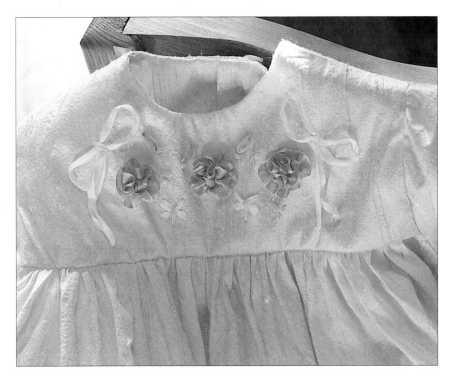

7 Using the pale lemon ribbon, work two Merrilyn bows with long twisted tails on either side of the work already stitched.

8 Sew the seed pearls in the center of the yellow flowers and at the base of the leaves.

9 On the center front of the skirt and approximately 6in/15cm up from the bottom, work three pre-gathered roses in the same colors and spaced as on the yoke. Work the yellow ribbon flowers, the green leaves, and the ivory embroidery floss flowers, then sew on the seed pearls as before.

10 Using chalk or pencil, draw two parallel lines as in the template below. Work along the line with the lemon ribbon in ribbon stitch to the end.

11 Sew a seed pearl at the top of each ribbon stitch.

12 Cut out and make up the dress according to the pattern instructions. I worked a looped button carrier to fit over the pearl buttons as a finishing touch.

FOUR GREETING CARDS

Silk ribbon embroidery is a perfect medium for hand-stitched greeting cards. I have given four designs here with specific uses; however all but the Christmas card could be mixed and matched for other occasions. Before mounting your work, you may like to put a small amount of batting at the back of the embroidery. This pads the work and makes for a better finish. The Christmas card has a simple little design, but it is quite quick and definitely fun to work. Instead of the more usual daffodils for the Mother's Day card, I thought some very simple irises would be good. I used green moiré taffeta as the background fabric, but other fabrics—linen, chintz, or silk dupioni—would work just as well. The wedding and birthday cards have both been mounted in specially cut cards with stenciled butterflies as an additional decoration. They could be displayed in store-bought frame with a 3in/8cm square aperture.

YOU WILL NEED

Christmas card

Piece of cream silk to fit the
    card mount plus a small overlap

2¼yd/2m each of three
    different shades of 4mm green
    silk ribbon

8 bright beads in Christmas
    colors

Beading needle

Sewing thread for beads

Scrap of 3mm gold ribbon

Card mount

Mother's Day card

1 piece of green taffeta to fit the
    card mount plus a small overlap

20in/51cm 3mm blue-purple
    silk ribbon

Crewel or similar needle

Matching green embroidery floss

30in/76cm 3mm green silk
    ribbon

Card mount

Wedding card

Piece of cream silk to fit the
    card mount plus a small overlap

30in/76cm 4mm tan silk
    ribbon

30in/76cm 7mm orange silk
    ribbon

30in/76cm 7mm green silk
    ribbon

30in/76cm 4mm pale green
    silk ribbon

Length of tan embroidery floss

Crewel or similar needle

1 card mount

or

Piece of cardboard, 20 x 6in/
    51 x 15cm

Butterfly stamp (optional)

Variegated stamp ink pad
    (optional)

Embossing powder (optional)

Heat gun (optional)

Birthday card

Piece of green satin to fit the
    card mount plus a small overlap

20in/51cm 4mm pale orange
    silk ribbon

Scrap of pale 4mm brown silk
    ribbon

10in/25cm 7mm orange silk
   ribbon
10in/25cm 7mm dull green
   silk ribbon
Length of yellow embroidery
   floss
Crewel or similar needle
Card mount
or
Piece of cardboard, 20 x 6in/
   51 x 15cm
Butterfly stamp (optional)
Variegated stamp ink pad
   (optional)
Embossing powder (optional)
Heat gun (optional)

All cards
No. 18 chenille needle
Small amount of batting
   (optional)
5in/13cm embroidery hoop
Tailor's chalk or dressmaker's
   marking pencil
Fabric glue

To stitch the Christmas card

1 Make a template from the
  Christmas tree shape on page
97 and draw the outline onto the
center of the fabric with chalk or
pencil. Stretch the fabric on a hoop.

2 Using one green ribbon at a
  time, work French knots scat-
tered randomly over the whole tree
shape. Work from top to bottom
and avoid having too many lengths
of connecting ribbons between
stitches at the back of the work.

3 When the whole area of the
  tree has been worked, stitch the
beads at the ends of the branches.

4 Using the gold ribbon, stitch a
  triangle of three straight stitches at the top of the tree. Your work
is now ready to mount as described
below.

NOTES AND TIPS

It is essential that you work the
Christmas tree design on a hoop or
you may get puckering.

To stitch the Mother's Day card

1 Mark the center of the fabric with tailor's chalk or pencil and stretch it on a hoop.

2 Position the first flower head about ¾ in/2cm up from the center point. Work the flower using the blue-purple ribbon. First, make a lazy daisy stitch about ⅜ in/1cm in size. Take the needle to the back of the work and bring it out again below and to the right of the bottom of the lazy daisy stitch. Pass behind the lazy daisy stitch, using the eye of the needle first (to avoid catching the ribbon), then go back down into the fabric below and to the left of the lazy daisy.

3 Work a second flower head either to the right or to the left of the first, placing it at a slightly different height to add interest. Make a flower bud by just working one simple straight stitch.

4 With two strands of the embroidery floss, work the stalks in long straight stitches, taking them ¾in/2cm below the center mark.

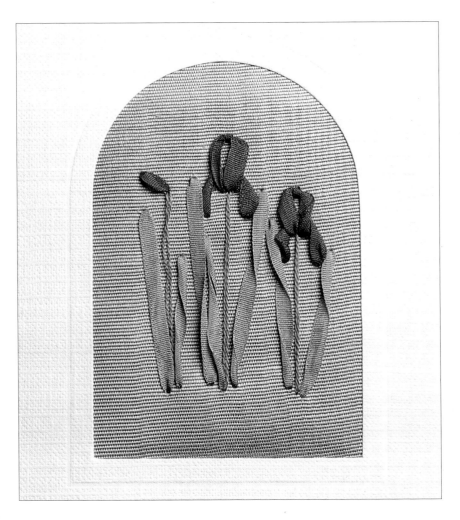

5 Use the green ribbon to work the leaves in long straight stitches, allowing the ribbon to twist to add more dimension to your work.

6 The embroidery is now ready to mount in its card, as described on page 96.

To stitch the wedding card

1 Make a template from the butterfly shape given on page 97 and draw the outline onto the center of the fabric using tailor's chalk or pencil. Alternatively, draw your own butterfly shape. Stretch the fabric on a hoop.

2 Using the tan ribbon, work the body of the butterfly in a whipped running stitch.

3 Change to the orange ribbon and work the outer half of the right wing in straight stitches of varying lengths but working to the drawn shape of the outer wing.

4 Change back to the tan ribbon and work again in straight stitches of varying lengths from the body up to the orange stitches.

5 Work the left wing of the butterfly in the same way, using the 7mm green ribbon for the outer part and the 3mm pale green ribbon for the inner.

6 Using two strands of embroidery floss, work two pistil stitches for the feelers.

7 The card is now ready to mount. For a store-bought mount, follow the instructions below. If you cut your own, trace the leaf template on page 97 onto the left half of the middle section of the card and cut it out. Mount the embroidery as described below.

8 To add the cut-out butterflies, work as follows: Using the butterfly stamp and ink pad, stamp the card to the right of the embroidery. Repeat in the right-hand corner of the card.

9 Stamp a spare piece of card, then sprinkle with embossing powder. Use a heat gun to produce a raised shine. Repeat.

NOTES AND TIPS

To match the colors of the stencil ink, the colors of the ribbon were chosen after the stenciling was completed.

10 Cut out the two butterflies, glue just the body section and stick them over the previously stamped butterflies.

To stitch the birthday card

1 Mark the center of the fabric with tailor's chalk or pencil and stretch it on a hoop.

2 Using the pale orange silk ribbon, work a straight stitch at the center point, then a series of other straight stitches in the positions shown in the stitch diagram opposite.

3 Next, work a five-petal flower in ribbon stitch in the position shown in the diagram.

4 Change to the pale brown ribbon and work a couple of buds, using straight stitch as shown.

5 With the orange ribbon, work two ribbon stitches as shown.

6 Use two strands of the yellow embroidery floss to work a straight stitch up the center of the two orange petals.

7 Mark a point approximately ¾in/2cm below the center. Using two strands of the green embroidery floss, work stalks in straight stitch and bring them down to the point just marked. Join the foliage stems with a large back stitch and work fly stitch with a straight stitch into the petals to form the calyxes.

8 Using the green ribbon, work four ribbon stitch leaves to cover the base of the stalks.

9 Mount the card as described for the wedding card above.

⬭	Straight stitch
🐟	Ribbon stitch
⋎	Fly stitch and straight stitch
○	Bead

To make all the cards

1 Place the card mount face up and opened out. Slide the embroidery underneath the opening until the design is central. Mark the edges of the card on the fabric. Remove the fabric and trim it back ⅛in/3mm beyond the marked lines so that no fabric can be seen at the edges of the card.

2 Glue the reverse of the card opening and all over the back of the right-hand flap. Place the fabric back in position and make sure it is taut. If you use the batting,

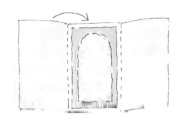

trim it to fit over the opening and put it in place. Fold over the right-hand flap (see diagram). Press until the glue holds firm but be careful not to flatten the embroidery.

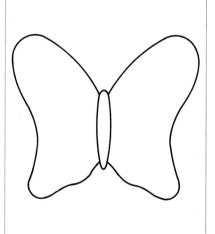

PICTURE BOW

Picture bows draw attention to a favorite photograph or painting and add a nice decorative touch to the furnishings of the room as well. Choose a color that will match both the picture and the interior decoration. I chose an aqua silk in keeping with the beach scene and thought it would also be interesting to theme the work on the bow tails with the picture it is going to display.

YOU WILL NEED

1yd/1m aqua silk dupioni, 45in/114cm wide

Tailor's chalk or dressmaker's marking pencil

Embroidery hoop

No. 18 chenille needle

Crewel or similar needle

Skein medium coral embroidery floss

40in/1m 7mm light coral silk ribbon

20in/51cm 7mm dark coral silk ribbon

Length of dark coral embroidery floss

Aqua sewing thread

I curtain ring for hanging

To stitch the design

1 Cut two strips, 7in/18cm wide and to the length required. These make the tails for the bow and so will stretch from the bow above the picture and hang beneath it. Make a template from the shell shape on page 101 and transfer it to the end of one of the bow tails, 4¾in/12cm from the base and 1in/2.5cm from the left-hand edge, using either tailor's chalk or pencil. Stretch this area on an embroidery hoop.

2 Using two strands of the medium coral embroidery floss, work in satin stitch to block the area shown in the stitch diagram opposite.

3 Change to the light coral ribbon and work the area shown in straight stitch. Do not allow the ribbon to twist but do work fairly loosely so that the ribbon curls.

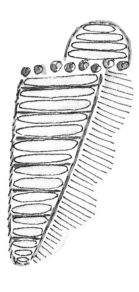

⌒	Stem stitch
⬭	Straight stitch (ribbon)
⌒	Back stitch
⊚	French knot
▨	Satin stitch

4 Using the dark coral ribbon, work the area shown with double-wrap loose French knots.

5 Change to the dark coral embroidery floss and work the center line of the shell in backstitch, using two strands only. With the same thread, work long straight stitches across the light coral ribbon. To finish off, still using the dark coral embroidery floss, stitch along the outside edge of the light coral ribbon in stem stitch.

6 Repeat the embroidery on the second bow tail, but reverse the template and position it 1in/2.5cm from the right-hand edge.

To make the bow

1 From the remaining silk, cut a piece 7½ x 23⅝ in/19 x 60cm on the bias. This is for the main part of the bow.

2 Fold lengthways with right sides together. Pin and machine stitch, taking a ⅜in/1cm seam allowance. Turn right side out so that the seam is in the middle of one side.

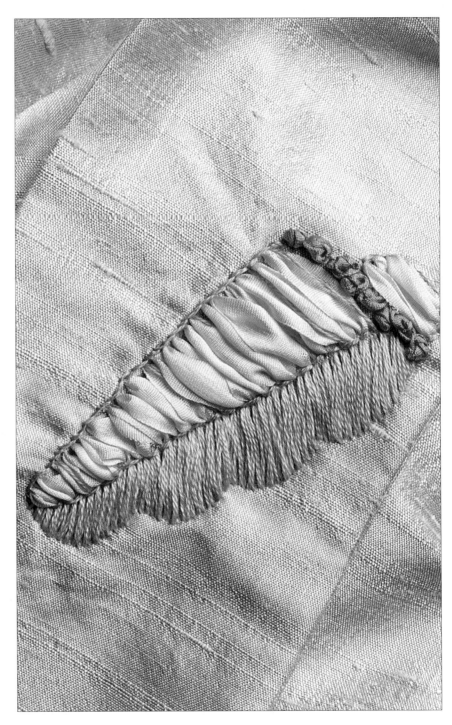

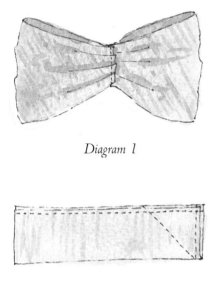

Diagram 1

Diagram 2

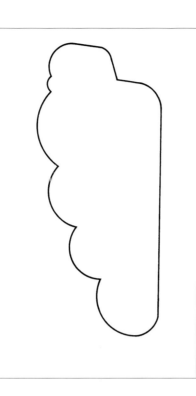

If you decide to work your own design, keep it fairly simple, so that it complements the picture on display and is not over-bearing.

3 Fold the ends into the middle to make the bow, then pleat and secure by hand (see Diagram 1).

4 Cut a small piece of the silk, approximately 2½ x 4¾in/6 x 12cm and hem all sides. Gather at each short end and fold around the center of the bow; pull in the middle slightly. Secure by hand at the back of the bow.

5 Fold the two strips for the bow tails in half lengthways, right sides together, and machine stitch down the long side and the bottom short side, ⅜in/1cm from the edge.

Form the pointed bottom by stitching a line from the bottom folded edge to 3⅛in/8cm of the way up the seamed edge (see Diagram 2). Trim the excess fabric at the corner.

6 Turn right side out and press. Pleat the top end of the tails, then stitch behind the bow by hand. Finally, stitch a curtain ring to the back of the bow for hanging.

ℱOLK QUILT SAMPLER

I have seen many small patchwork samplers hung on the walls of houses in the States and have always thought they provide a feeling of warmth and friendliness. This has inspired me to create an American-style folk art sampler in ribbons on a natural muslin background. The motifs are not complicated to stitch, and making this sampler is very good practice for keeping straight stitches straight.

YOU WILL NEED

Piece of muslin, 12 x 12in/ 30 x 30cm

Embroidery hoop or frame

Tailor's chalk or dressmaker's marking pencil

No. 18 chenille needle

Crewel or similar needle

40in/1m 4mm yellow silk ribbon

1²⁄₃yd/1.5m 4mm blue silk ribbon

2¼yd/2m 4mm red silk ribbon

1²⁄₃yd/1.5m 4mm green silk ribbon

40in/1m 4mm purple silk ribbon

Yellow embroidery floss

Red embroidery floss

Black embroidery floss

Scrap of 7mm green silk ribbon

20in/51cm 4mm brown silk ribbon

30in/76cm 4mm burnt orange silk ribbon

40in/1m 7mm yellow silk ribbon

Green embroidery floss

20in/51cm 13mm green silk ribbon

Piece of lightweight batting, 10¼ x 10³⁄₄in/26 x 27cm

Piece of border and backing fabric, 16 x 24in/41 x 61cm

2 lengths of ¼in/6mm dowel, 13in/33cm long

1yd/1m cord or ribbon for hanging

To stitch the design

1 Mark a grid of nine blocks onto the muslin, with the vertical lines 2½in/6.5cm apart and horizontal lines 2⁵⁄₈in/7cm apart. Stretch on an embroidery hoop or frame.

2 Using the heart-shaped template on page 106, draw five hearts onto the fabric in the positions shown in the stitch diagram on page 104.

3 Utilize the chicken template on page 106 to draw two chickens onto the fabric. Leave the remaining two squares blank.

4 Work each heart in straight stitch, using the colors of 4mm ribbon shown on the stitch diagram and keeping the tension firm and even.

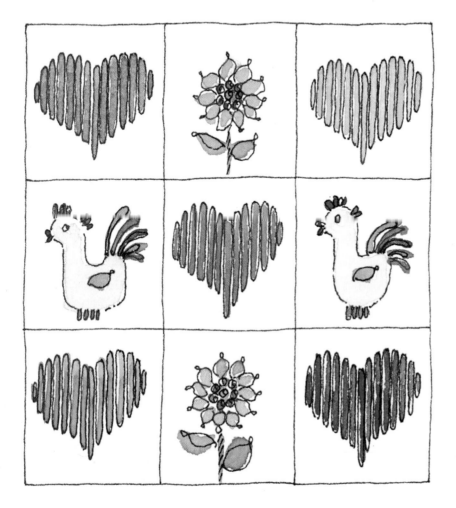

Straight stitch	
Ribbon stitch	
French knot	
Stem stitch	

6 With the blue, red, and green 4mm ribbons, work the tails in ribbon stitch, as described on page 17 but with a single twist in the ribbon. Keep the tension fairly loose to produce a nicely curved stitch.

7 Work the eye, using two strands of black embroidery floss in one French knot. Finish the chicken by working the wing in the middle of the body in ribbon stitch using the 7mm green ribbon.

8 For the sunflowers, use brown silk ribbon and work one central French knot followed by two rounds of French knots. Using the burnt orange ribbon, go around once more with French knots.

9 With the yellow 7mm silk ribbon, work ribbon stitches all around the circle.

10 Use two strands of green embroidery floss to work the stalk in stem stitch.

11 Stitch the leaves, using green 13mm ribbon and working in ribbon stitch.

Make sure that the stitches are close together so that they overlap slightly to form a solid block of color.

5 Stitch the chickens with three strands of yellow embroidery floss in both long and short straight stitches, worked horizontally and vertically, following the shape of the body. Using red ribbon, work the combs and legs in small straight stitches. Stitch the beaks, using two strands of red embroidery floss working in straight stitch.

To make the sampler

1 Place the batting on the wrong side of the muslin and pin it in place. Machine-stitch together along the marked grid lines.

2 Cut two pieces from the border and backing fabric, each 3⅛ x 12in/9 x 30cm. Machine-stitch to either side of the sampler, right sides together, along the outer vertical grid line. Open out and press.

3 Cut another piece from the border and backing fabric, 3⅛ x 16½in/8 x 42cm, and machine-stitch to the bottom of the sampler, with right sides together along the bottom horizontal grid line. Open out and press (see Diagram 1).

4 Cut another piece from the border and backing fabric, 14½ x 16½in/37 x 42cm, and place it over the top of the embroidery, with right sides together. Machine-stitch along the top horizontal grid line and across the side pieces. Press.

5 Fold back the side panels so that they measure 1⅜in/3.5cm and pin. Fold back the top and bottom panels so that they measure 1⅜in/3.5cm and pin.

6 Turn under the backing piece to fit the front and press. Machine-stitch across the top and bottom of the sampler, 1⅜in/3.5cm away from the top and bottom horizontal grid lines to form ⅝in/1.5cm channels for the dowel rods (see Diagram 2).

7 Slipstitch the back and front of the sampler down the sides, but leave the top and bottom channels free.

8 Insert the dowel rods into the top and bottom channels and tie a length of cord or ribbon to either end of the top dowel in order to hang the sampler.

Diagram 1

Diagram 2

ROSE GIFT BOX

Trinket boxes are always nice presents to give and to receive. The construction of this box is the same as that of the silk box on page 79, but this one is made in a pretty cotton fabric appropriate for a birthday or perhaps a Mother's Day offering. The pattern I have worked can be color-matched with any small floral print fabric.

YOU WILL NEED

Tailor's chalk or dressmaker's
   marking pencil
Piece of cream cotton fabric,
   10 x 10in/25 x 25cm, for the
   lid inset
5in/13cm embroidery hoop or
   frame
No. 18 chenille needle
Crewel or similar needle
20in/51cm 4mm dark pink silk
   ribbon
20in/51cm 4mm medium pink
   silk ribbon
20in/51cm 4mm green silk
   ribbon
Matching green embroidery floss
Stiff paper or template plastic
Sharp craft knife
Thin cardboard, approximately
   1/8in/3mm thick
Piece of felt, 17 x 10in/
   43 x 25cm

Piece of floral print cotton
   fabric, 18 x 12in/46 x 30cm
   for the outside of the box
Fabric glue and narrow glue brush
Cream sewing thread
Curved needle
1 piece of plain color cotton
   fabric, 24 x 12in/
   61 x 30cm, for the box
   lining
Circle of batting, 3in/8cm
   in diameter

To stitch and make the design

1 Draw a 3in/8cm circle in the center of the inset fabric. Stretch the fabric on an embroidery hoop or frame.

2 Using dark pink ribbon, work the rosebud in two back-to-back side ribbon stitches in the position shown in the stitch diagram on page 108.

3 With the same ribbon, work three lazy daisy stitches in the positions marked. Fill in the center of these stitches with single straight stitches, to work a blocked lazy daisy.

4 With the medium pink ribbon, work in fishbone stitch for each rose, and put three stitches on either side of the blocked lazy daisy.

5 Using the dark pink ribbon, work one or two straight stitches to each rose. Tuck them behind the petals already worked.

6 Use the green ribbon to work ribbon stitch leaves in the positions shown.

7 Utilizing two strands of the embroidery floss and working in stem stitch, work the stalks of the roses as shown.

8 Make up the box following the instructions and using the templates given on pages 78 to 82.

Side ribbon stitch
Ribbon stitch
Blocked lazy daisy
Fishbone stitch
Stem stitch
Straight stitch

NOTES AND TIPS

I recommend that you use a cotton fabric for box-making; it is firm and does not fray too badly.

SPIRAL TOPIARY TREE

Over the centuries topiary trees have remained popular, and there is nothing I like better than to see an avenue of beautifully clipped box evergreens in a stately home garden. I have created two tree shapes, both on a cream damask background and identically framed so that they can be worked either singly or as a pair. This first spiral tree is a medium-level project stitched largely in French knots. The light and dark sections of the spiral are both worked in two colors to give a realistic shading to the tree.

YOU WILL NEED
Piece of cream damask,
   16 x 16in/41 x 41cm
Tailor's chalk or dressmaker's
   marking pencil
Embroidery hoop or frame
No. 18 chenille needle
20in/51cm 4mm brown silk
   ribbon
6¾yd/6m 4mm light green
   silk ribbon
6¾yd/6m 4mm medium
   green silk ribbon
2¼yd/2m 4mm very dark
   green silk ribbon
1⅔yd/1.5m 4mm dark green
   silk ribbon
1⅔yd/1.5m 7mm gold silk
   ribbon
20in/51cm 7mm cream silk
   ribbon

10in/25cm 7mm green silk
   ribbon
Length of green embroidery
   floss
20in/51cm 4mm pale blue
   silk ribbon
Length of yellow embroidery
   floss
10in/25cm 4mm green
   silk ribbon

To stitch the design

1 Transfer the template on page 113 to the center of the fabric. Press the fabric well, then stretch on a hoop or frame.

2 Using the brown ribbon, stitch the sections of the trunk first in a twisted chain stitch.

3 Next, take the light green ribbon and starting at the top of the tree, work French knots within the first section. Dot them about, leaving spaces in between. Fill these with French knots worked with the medium green ribbon. The knots do not have to cover the surface completely; it's fine if small areas of fabric show through.

4 With the very dark green ribbon, work in the same way in the second section, filling in with dark green. I have stitched slightly more very dark green knots to achieve an overall darker shade.

5 Continue down the tree in this way, alternating one section worked in the two lighter greens with one in the dark greens. Finish with a section in the lighter greens.

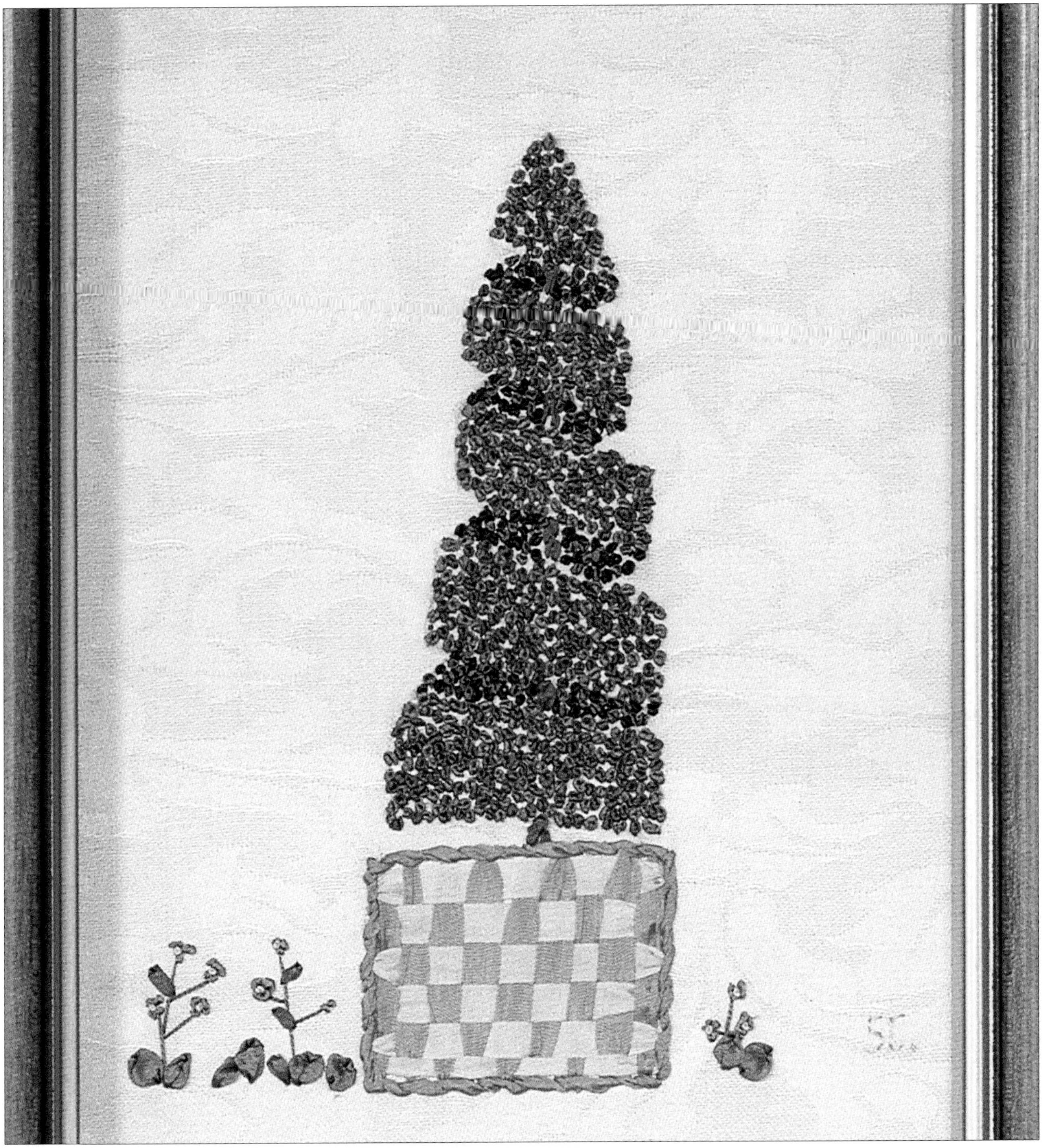

6 To make the basket, first work the gold ribbon in long straight vertical stitches from the top to the bottom of the rectangle. Then make horizontal straight stitches with the cream ribbon, weaving them under and over the gold ribbon.

7 To neaten the edges, stitch around all four sides of the basket in a whipped running stitch, using the gold ribbon.

8 Work the detail at the base of the basket as follows: Work loop stitch flowers in the pale blue ribbon with a yellow embroidery floss French knot in the center. Work pairs of ribbon stitch leaves level with the base, using the 7mm green ribbon. Stitch the stalks using two strands of green embroidery floss in straight stitch. Then work one or two ribbon stitch leaves with the 4mm green ribbon.

9 Have the embroidery framed by a professional framer. The damask should be stretched onto an acid-free backing board before being mounted in the frame. I have chosen a box frame for this and the following project.

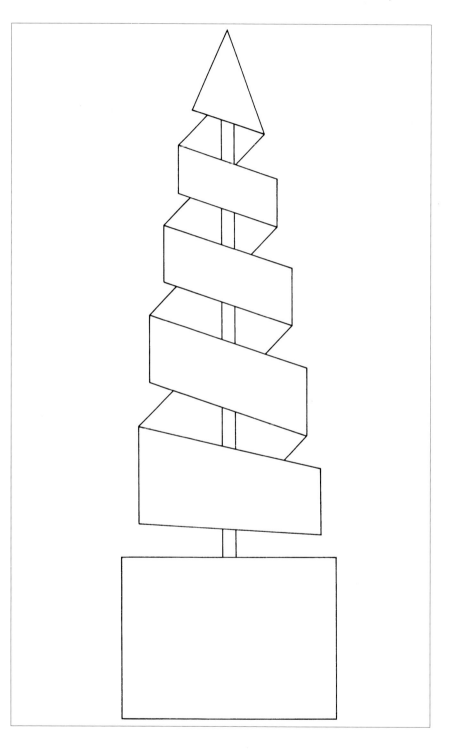

ROUND TOPIARY TREE

This design uses a variety of stitches worked all over the surface to produce an alternative topiary design as a twin to the previous project. This is a more advanced design for the practiced silk ribbon embroiderer. It can be adapted to any color scheme and would also look good on a cushion front.

YOU WILL NEED
Piece of cream damask,
  16 x 16in/41 x 40cm
Embroidery hoop or frame
Tailor's chalk or dressmaker's
  marking pencil
No. 18 chenille needle
Crewel or similar needle
40in/1m 4mm off-white silk
  ribbon
1²⁄₃yd/1.5m 4mm red silk
  ribbon
Length of mauve embroidery
  floss
20in/51cm 4mm mauve silk
  ribbon
Mustard embroidery floss
40in/1m 4mm purple silk
  ribbon
20in/51cm 4mm yellow silk
  ribbon
1²⁄₃yd/1.5m 4mm blue silk
  ribbon

Gold embroidery floss
2¼yd/2.3m 7mm gold silk
  ribbon
Green embroidery floss to
  match the leaves
1²⁄₃yd/1.5m 4mm moss green
  silk ribbon
20in/51cm 7mm green silk
  ribbon
40in/1m 4mm medium green
  silk ribbon
20in/51cm 4mm brown silk
  ribbon
20in/51cm 7mm cream silk
  ribbon

To stitch the design

1 Press the fabric well. Mark the center of the fabric with two crossed pins, then draw a 3in/8cm diameter circle centrally on the fabric so that its base rests on the center mark. Remove the pins.

2 Draw a vertical line 2¼in/5.5cm long from the base of the circle. This marks the position of the trunk. Draw a rectangle at the bottom of the trunk line, 2¾in/7cm wide and 1¾in/4.5cm deep to form the basket. Stretch the marked area on an embroidery hoop or frame.

3 Work the design in the circle with the various silk ribbons and two strands of embroidery floss as indicated on the stitch diagram on page 116. Move from largest to smallest flowers, then fill in with

	Whipped running stitch
	Twisted chain stitch
	Coral stitch
	French knot
	Loop stitch
	Spider web rose
	Pistil stitch
	Lazy daisy stitch
	Ribbon stitch
	Fly stitch and straight stitch

lazy daisy and ribbon stitch leaves, making sure that the whole area is richly filled.

The flowers are worked as follows:

Red flowers—three off-white French knots in the center, surrounded by red coral stitch.

Mauve flowers—spider web roses.

Purple flowers—French knot in mustard embroidery floss in the center with five ribbon stitch petals in purple.

Blue flowers—French knot in yellow ribbon in the center surrounded by four to six blue French knots.

White flowers—French knot in gold embroidery floss in the center, surrounded by five loop stitches in off-white with pistil stitch in gold embroidery floss on each loop.

Yellow buds—ribbon stitch in gold

ribbon with detail in two strands of green embroidery floss.

4 Work leaves as follows: Around the blue flowers in lazy daisy stitch, using moss green ribbon. Around the mauve flowers in puffed ribbon stitch, using 7mm green ribbon. Around the purple flowers in ribbon stitch using 4mm medium green ribbon.

5 Stitch the tree trunk in twisted chain stitch using 4mm brown ribbon.

6 Work the basket with the 7mm gold and cream ribbons as described on page 113 (Step 6).

7 To neaten the edges, stitch around all four sides of the basket in a whipped running stitch with the gold ribbon.

8 To finish off, add a few flowers and leaves at the top of the basket and a few leaves at the bottom on the ground as shown in the stitch diagram.

9 For framing, see the comments on page 113 (step 9).

FLOWER GARDEN SAMPLER

On this quilted sampler, I have embroidered some of my favorite flowers. Some of them I grow in my garden, and others I can only dream of growing! This is a complex project, suitable for an experienced embroiderer. The flowers are each shown and described separately and could of course be used in all sorts of other ways to embellish other projects. The ribbons for each flower are listed separately.

YOU WILL NEED

Piece of muslin, 34½ x 17in/ 87.3 x 43cm

Tailor's chalk or dressmaker's marking pencil

Embroidery hoop or frame

No. 18 chenille needle

Crewel or similar needle

Piece of lightweight batting, 15 x 15½in/38 x 39.5cm

3¾yd/3.5m 3mm dark green satin ribbon

Sewing thread to match ribbon and muslin

2 lengths of ⅜in/1cm dowel, each 19in/48cm long

24in/61cm ribbon or cord for hanging

Pansies

20in/51cm 7mm purple silk ribbon

20in/51cm 7mm blue silk ribbon

10in/25cm 2mm yellow silk ribbon

Length of navy blue embroidery floss

Length of green embroidery floss

20in/51cm 7mm dark green silk ribbon

Lavender

1yd/.9m 2mm lavender silk ribbon

Length of pale green pearl cotton

10in/25cm 2mm light green silk ribbon

Cyclamen

20in/51cm 7mm white silk ribbon

Length of cerise embroidery floss

Length of yellow embroidery floss

Length of dark green embroidery floss

10in/25cm 7mm dark green silk ribbon

Forget-me-nots

30in/76cm 2mm blue silk ribbon

Length of green embroidery floss

Length of yellow embroidery floss

20in/51cm 7mm green silk ribbon

Primroses/Auriculas

20in/51cm 4mm dark pink embroidery floss

Length of yellow embroidery floss

Length of green embroidery floss

10in/25cm 7mm green silk ribbon

Arum lilies
20in/51cm 13mm white silk
  ribbon
20in/51cm 7mm green silk
  ribbon
Length of green embroidery
  floss
Length of yellow embroidery
  floss

Chrysanthemums
10in/25cm 4mm deep red silk
  ribbon
30in/76cm 4mm tan silk
  ribbon
Length of green embroidery
  floss

Irises
20in/51cm 4mm blue-purple
  silk ribbon
Length of green embroidery
  floss
20in/51cm 4mm green silk
  ribbon

Roses
20in/51cm 4mm light pink silk
  ribbon
20in/51cm 4mm medium pink
  silk ribbon
20in/51cm 4mm very light
  green silk ribbon

Length of very light green
  embroidery floss

Daisies
20in/51cm 4mm yellow silk
  ribbon
Length of yellow embroidery
  floss
Length of light green
  embroidery floss
20in/51cm 4mm lime green
  silk ribbon

Violets
20in/51cm 4mm purple silk
  ribbon
Length of yellow embroidery
  floss
Length of green embroidery floss
20in/51cm 7mm green silk
  ribbon

Lilies of the valley
20in/51cm 4mm white silk
  ribbon
Length of dark green
  embroidery floss
20in/51cm 7mm dark green
  silk ribbon

Hollyhocks
1⅔yd/1.5m 4mm claret silk
  ribbon

Length of dark green
  embroidery floss
20in/51cm 7mm dark green
  silk ribbon
Length of light pink embroidery
  floss

Snowdrops
20in/51cm 4mm white silk
  ribbon
Length of green embroidery
  floss

Red-hot pokers
20in/51cm 4mm yellow silk
  ribbon
40in/1m 4mm orange silk
  ribbon
Length of green embroidery
  floss
20in/51cm 4mm green silk
  ribbon

Bluebells
20in/51cm 4mm pink/purple
  silk ribbon
Length of medium green
  embroidery floss to match
  ribbon
20in/51cm 4mm medium green
  silk ribbon

To stitch the design

At one end of the fabric, mark out a grid of 16 squares, each measuring 3¼in/8.3cm square, positioned 4in/10cm up from the lower short edge and 2¼in/5.7cm in from each long side. Stretch the muslin on a hoop or frame and work from top to bottom of the sampler, placing the flowers as shown in the key on page 126.

Pansies

1 Starting at the top left-hand square, work the group of pansies as follows:

2 Using the purple ribbon, for each flower work two ribbon stitches and one for the bud positioned as shown in the photograph.

3 Change to the blue ribbon and work three ribbon stitches per flower.

4 With the yellow ribbon, work a small straight stitch into each of the bottom three petals.

5 Use two strands of the navy blue embroidery floss to work three straight stitches onto the yellow stitches and a sizable French knot into the center of the flower.

6 Stitch the three stalks, using two strands of green embroidery floss in straight stitch.

7 Work the leaves, utilizing green ribbon in ribbon stitch.

Lavender

1 Using the lavender ribbon, work in small straight stitches in a fern shape as shown in the photograph to form the flower heads. Whip each of the straight stitches, in the same way as for whipped running stitch (see page 24).

2 With the pale green pearl cotton, work the four stalks in straight stitch.

3 Use the green silk ribbon to work the leaves in small straight stitches at either side of the stems.

Cyclamen

1 Using the white ribbon, work the flower heads positioned as shown in the photograph. Each flower has three petals. Work the petals in straight stitch.

2 With two strands of the cerise embroidery floss, work a straight stitch from the bottom of each petal to about a third of the way up.

3 Use two strands of the yellow embroidery floss to work a single horizontal stitch along the bottom of each flower head.

4 Using two strands of the green embroidery floss, work the stems of the three flowers in stem stitch as shown.

5 The leaves are worked using the green silk ribbon in long ribbon stitch.

Forget-me-nots

1 With the blue ribbon, work the flower petals in small straight stitches. All the main flowers have five petals, but it will look more natural if you work some with just one or two.

2 Work the stems in straight stitch with two strands of the green emboidery floss and join three or four flower heads to each main stem.

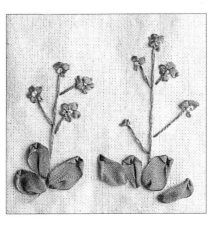

3 To work a French knot in the center of each flower head, use two strands of the yellow embroidery floss.

4 Using the green ribbon, work the clusters of leaves in ribbon stitch. Be sure you remember to work some of the leaves diagonally across the stems as shown in the photograph above.

Primroses / Auriculas

1 Use the dark pink ribbon to work the flower petals in French knots and vary the number of knots in each cluster.

2 Using two strands of the yellow embroidery floss, work a single wrap French knot in the center of each flower head.

3 With two strands of the green embroidery floss, work the stems in stem stitch.

4 Work the leaves with the green ribbon in ribbon stitch clusters.

Arum lilies

1 Use the white ribbon to work the flower heads as a single ribbon stitch.

2 Using the green ribbon, work the leaves in ribbon stitch close to the flower heads.

3 Use two strands of the green embroidery floss to work the stems in long straight stitch.

4 With one strand of the yellow embroidery floss, work small French knots up the center of each flower head about halfway up the white stitches.

Chrysanthemums

1 Work three French knots for each flower head, using the deep red ribbon.

2 Work two rounds of coral stitch in the tan ribbon for each flower.

3 Utilize two strands of the green embroidery floss to work the stems in stem stitch and the leaves in fly stitch.

Irises

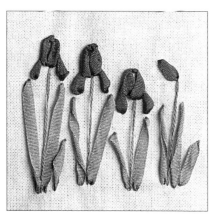

1 Using the blue-purple ribbon, work the flowers by first making a lazy daisy stitch. Then bring the needle up from underneath the fabric, pass the ribbon underneath the lazy daisy stitch and back down into the fabric at the other side (see Stitch Library, page 19).

2 Use two strands of the green embroidery floss to work the flower stems in long straight stitch.

3 Work the leaves in long twisted straight stitch with the green ribbon.

Roses

1 With fishbone stitch, work the rose flowers with the light and medium pink ribbon. Use the medium pink for the center stitch, then two light pink stitches followed by two medium pink. The flower bud has just two back-to-back ribbon stitches in medium pink as shown in the photograph.

2 Work the leaves all around the flowers in ribbon stitch, using the green ribbon.

3 With two strands of the green embroidery floss, work the stems in stem stitch.

4 Sew the odd leaf or two across the stem in small ribbon stitches as in the photograph.

Daisies

1 With the yellow ribbon, work the flower petals in ribbon stitch in a circle of seven petals.

2 Using two strands of the yellow embroidery floss, work two or three double-wrap French knots in the center of each flower head.

3 Work the stems in stem stitch, using two strands of the green embroidery floss.

4 Use the green ribbon to work the leaves across the stem in short straight stitches.

Violets

1 Using the purple ribbon, work five petals for each flower head in ribbon stitch. Leave a definite gap between the top two petals and the bottom three petals.

2 With two strands of the yellow embroidery floss, work one double-wrap French knot in the center of each flower.

3 Using two strands of the green embroidery floss, work the stems in long straight stitches.

4 Use the green ribbon to work the leaves in ribbon stitch. Make the leaves quite puffy.

Lilies of the valley

1 With the white ribbon, work the flowers in curved rows of about four French knots.

2 Using two strands of the green embroidery floss, work the stems in stem stitch and straight stitch.

3 Work the leaves in long ribbon stitch, using the green ribbon.

4 With just one strand of the green embroidery floss, work a small running stitch up the center of each leaf.

Hollyhocks

I Using the claret ribbon, work four loose double-wrap French knots for the bottom of each flower. Work up the flower, increasing the tension of the knots, and after two or three rows work in single-wrap knots (follow the photograph for the shape of the flower). When you reach the top, just work two or three small straight stitches.

2 With two strands of the green embroidery floss, work one or two single lazy daisy stitches at the top of the flower for buds.

3 Use the green ribbon to work the leaves in puffed ribbon stitch at the base of each flower that points downward and one or two up the sides of the flowers.

4 With two strands of the pink embroidery floss, work French knots on top of the ribbon French knots here and there.

Snowdrops

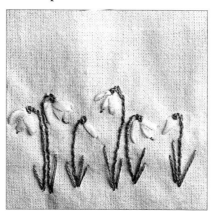

I Use the white ribbon to work three small straight stitches for each flower head, making the flowers hang downward. Work a couple of buds with just one stitch, as shown in the photograph.

2 Using two strands of the green embroidery floss, work the stems in stem stitch, then work the leaves in medium-length straight stitches.

Red-hot pokers

I With the yellow ribbon, work three straight stitches, which will form the bottom of each of the flowers. Then work a French knot at the end of each of these straight stitches.

2 Using the orange ribbon, work the rest of the flower petals in the same way to form a longish rectangular shape as shown in the photograph.

3 With two strands of the green embroidery floss, work the stems in stem stitch.

4 Work the leaves in long twisted straight stitch, using the green ribbon. The left-hand flower has three leaves, the right two.

Bluebells

1 Using the pink-purple ribbon, work sets of three ribbon stitches for the flower head, just pulling the ribbon through until you get a rolled edge.

2 Using two strands of the green embroidery floss, work the stems in stem stitch.

3 With the green ribbon, work the leaves (two on either side of the flower head in straight stitch and one at the bottom of the stem in ribbon stitch).

To make the sampler

1 Place the square of batting behind the embroidered muslin. Baste the two layers together thoroughly to avoid puckering when you are mahine-stitching.

2 Stitch lengths of dark green satin ribbon along the grid lines on the front of the muslin, using a machine zigzag stitch and tucking the raw ends underneath. Remove the basting threads.

3 Fold back the sides and top and bottom of the muslin around the embroidery so that there is a plain border of 2¼in/5.7cm at top and bottom and 1½in/4cm at each side. Fold under the raw edges of the muslin at the back of the embroidery so that they are just out of sight from the front. Pin, then machine-stitch across the top edge ¾in/2cm from the top to make a channel for the dowel. Do the same at the bottom.

4 Hem the back to the front, leaving the channel sides open. Remove the pins. Insert the dowel rods and tie on the cord or ribbon for hanging.

pansies	lavender	cyclamen	forget-me-nots
primroses/auriculas	arum lilies	chrysan-themums	irises
roses	daisies	violets	lilies-of-the-valley
hollyhocks	snowdrops	red hot pokers	bluebells

INDEX

arum lilies 122
auriculas 122
back stitch in embroidery
  floss 26
back-to-back ribbon stitch 18
barrel cushion 34
beads 11
birthday card 96
blocked lazy daisy stitch 19
bluebells 126
bullion rose 21
bullion stitch 21
chain stitch 19
chenille needle 10
Chinese linen blouse 67
christening gown 87
Christmas card 92
chrysanthemums 123
coral stitch 23
couched straight stitch 17
crewel needle 10
cushions
  barrel 34
  heart-shaped bed pillow 40
  lacy bed 37
  laurel wreath 30
  Thai silk 44
cyclamen 120
daisies 124
double-edged satin ribbons 11
double-edged satin rose 27
dressmaker's marking pencil 10
embroidery floss 11
embroidery frame 10
embroidery hoop 10
evening vest 73
evening wrap 70
fabrics 11
finishing off 13
fishbone stitch 24
flower garden sampler 118
fly stitch in embroidery
  floss 25
folk quilt sampler 102

forget-me-nots 122
four greeting cards 91
frame 10
French knot 21
gift box 77
gold thread 11
greeting cards 91
heart-shaped bed pillow 40
hollyhocks 125
hoop 10
irises 123
lacy bed cushion 37
laundering 12
laurel wreath cushion 30
lavender 120
lazy daisy stitch 19
lilies of the valley 124
loop stitch 22
making a tassel 13
man-made ribbons 11
Merrilyn bow 20
mother's day card 94
muslin 11
muslin hat 61
napkins 58
needles 10
  chenille 10
  crewel 10
padded picture frame 83
pansies 120
pelmet 53
pearl cotton 11
picture bow 98
picture frame 83
pillowcase 50
pinning ribbon 13
pins 10
pistil stitch 22
plastic clip frame 10
pre-gathered rose 25
primroses 122
quantities 11
red-hot pokers 125
ribbon stitch 17

ribbons 10
  double-edged satin 11
  man-made 11
  pure silk 10
  variegated 11
  wire-edged 11
rose gift box 107
roses 123
round topiary tree 114
samplers
  flower garden 118
  folk quilt 102
satin ribbons 11
satin stitch in embroidery
  floss 27
sheet 50
side ribbon stitch 18
silk ribbons 10
snowdrops 125
spider web rose 23
spiral topiary tree 110
starting off 12
stem stitch in embroidery
  floss 26
stitch diagrams 12
stitches
  back 26
  back-to-back ribbon 18
  bullion 21
  blocked lazy daisy 19
  chain 19
  coral 23
  couched straight 17
  fishbone 24
  fly 25
  French knot 21
  lazy daisy 19
  loop 22
  Merrilyn bow 20
  pistil 22
  pre-gathered rose 25
  ribbon 17
  satin 27
  side ribbon 18

stitches (cont.)
  spider web rose 23
  stem 26
  straight 16
  twisted chain 20
  whipped running 24
stitching beads 13
straight stitch 16
sunflower hatband 64
tablecloth 58
tailor's chalk 10
tapestry frame 10
tassels 13
templates 12
  christening gown 90
  Christmas card 97
  folk quilt 106
  gift box 81
  heart-shaped bed pillow 43
  leaf 97
  pelmet 54
  picture bow 101
  spiral topiary tree 113
  Thai silk cushion 49
  tieback 54
  wedding card 97
tension 13
Thai silk cushion 44
threads 11
  embroidery floss 11
  gold 11
  pearl cotton 11
tiebacks 53
topiary trees 110, 114
twisted chain stitch 20
variegated ribbons 11
violets 124
washing 12
wedding card 94
whipped running stitch 24
wire-edged ribbons 11

ACKNOWLEDGMENTS

The enjoyment I have had writing this book has been immeasurable. I have made a number of new friends and acquaintances, and I apologize if I fail to mention their names and I do appreciate everything they have done for me.

Various people have been of great help and have encouraged me. It is difficult to know in which order they should be thanked, but first and foremost must be Rosemary Wilkinson, who asked me to write this book, then throughout has shown me great patience and gentle encouragement. Second must be Jane Lang, a dear friend and extremely competent needlewoman. Jane did, from my sometimes very vague descriptions, turn all my embroidery into actual finished items. Despite having a young family, she always managed to finish projects within very tight deadlines. Thank you, Jane; I am indebted. Many thanks to Pat Garfield and Audrey Willows, two former students. Audrey produced the two gift boxes, and Pat designed and worked the butterfly cards; both are very competent ribbon embroiderers. To Enid Garner, who made the Evening Vest, thank you.

To my friend Helen, who helped me out on many occasions, taking my tribe of children despite the fact that she has a tribe of her own.

Lastly, to my family. My children were very enthusiastic about my work, and despite the fact that I had to labor solidly through the summer holiday, never once complained about the lack of outings. To my husband Richard, who never ceased believing in me even though I had doubts, my sincerest thanks.